SS

EINSATZGRUPPEN

NAZI DEATH SQUADS, 1939–1945

GERRY VAN TONDER

Pen & Sword
MILITARY

Liudmila Titova (Людмила Титова) was a Jewish-Ukrainian
poetess from Kiev, who wrote the epic poem 'Babi Yar'.

First published in Great Britain in 2018 by
PEN AND SWORD MILITARY
an imprint of
Pen and Sword Books Ltd
47 Church Street
Barnsley
South Yorkshire S70 2AS

Copyright © Gerry van Tonder, 2018

ISBN 978 1 526729 09 5

Typeset by Aura Technology and Software Services, India
Maps by George Anderson
Printed and bound in Malta by Gutenberg

Pen & Sword Books Ltd incorporates the imprints of Pen & Sword
Archaeology, Atlas, Aviation, Battleground, Discovery, Family History, History, Maritime,
Military, Naval, Politics, Railways, Select, Social History, Transport, True Crime, Claymore Press,
Frontline Books, Leo Cooper, Praetorian Press, Remember When, Seaforth Publishing and Wharncliffe.

For a complete list of Pen and Sword titles please contact
Pen and Sword Books Limited
47 Church Street, Barnsley, South Yorkshire, S70 2AS, England
email: enquiries@pen-and-sword.co.uk
website: www.pen-and-sword.co.uk

CONTENTS

MAJOR EINTSATZGRUPPEN MASSACRE SITES

TIMELINE

1921

September: The loose-knit, brown-shirted Saalschutzabteilung, or meeting hall protection detachment, of the German Labour Party, becomes informally known as the Sturmabteilung, or Storm Detachment (SA).

4 November: At a public meeting in the Munich Hofbräuhaus, elements of the SA beat up dissenters in the crowd. From this time, the SA title becomes official.

1925

9 November: Official formation date of the Schutzstaffel, or Protection Squad (SS).

1929

6 January: Adolf Hitler appoints Heinrich Himmler SS-Reichsführer.

1931

1 August: Reinhard Heydrich is made head of a newly created SS 'Ic Service' intelligence agency.

December: Heydrich is promoted to the rank of SS-Sturmbannführer.

1932

Himmler appoints Heydrich as chief of the Nazi Security Service, the Sicherheitsdienst (SD).

1933

30 January: Adolf Hitler, as chancellor, and the Nationalsozialist Deutsche Arbeiterpartei, or National Socialist German Labour Party (NSDAP), come to power in a coalition government.

3 February: Hitler reveals his *Lebensraum* programme.

15 March: Dachau Camp is established at an old gunpowder factory at this town near Munich.

26 June: Himmler takes Theodor Eicke out of a mental hospital and appoints him commandant of Dachau.

July: The Nazis are now in full control in Germany.

9 November: Himmler enhances the status of the SD to that of *amt* (office), and promotes Heydrich to the rank of Brigadeführer.

1934

22 April: Heydrich is appointed head of the Geheime Staatspolizei, or Gestapo, along with his position as chief of the SD.

9 June: The SD is designated the only SS and Nazi intelligence service.

30 June: Almost 200 critics of the NSDAP, including senior members of the SA, are rounded up and subsequently executed by SS death squads.

4 July: Eicke is placed in control of all concentration camps in the Reich. He creates Totenkopf, or Death's Head units, recruiting from within the ranks of the camp guards.

20 July: Hitler separates the SS from the Sturmabteilung.

14 December: Himmler reorganizes the SS into three departments: the SS-Verfügungstruppe, or Combat Support Force, comprising armed political squads, concentration camp guards, and the General SS for the remaining functions.

1936

10 February: The Gestapo is placed above the law.

1937

1 July: Himmler orders that all Jewish issues be handled by the SD.

1938

January: Himmler introduces a programme of incarcerating 'asocials', including the work-shy, gypsies, pimps and others unable to fit into the German community – the Four-Year Plan.

9–10 November: *Kristallnacht*, or Crystal Night, pogrom against all Jews in Nazi Germany.

8 December: Himmler issues a diktat that all matters relating to gypsies be dealt with on the basis of race.

1939

15 March: German troops invade Czechoslovakia and occupy Prague.

21 March: German troops enter Lithuania.

26 July: Heydrich's deputy, Adolf Eichmann, heads up the 'emigration' office for Jews in Prague.

1 September: Nazi Germany sends her troops into Poland; Heydrich forms the Einsatzgruppen to follow the invading German forces.

21 September: SS-Obergruppenführer Reinhard Heydrich instructs Einsatzgruppen commanders to give 'practical thought' to achieving the 'final aim'; Jewish ghettos are established in German-occupied Poland.

22–27 September: The SD and Sicherheitspolizei, or Security Police (SiPo), are merged to form the Reichssicherheitshauptamt, or Reich Main Security Office (RSHA), headed by Heydrich. Jewish ghettos are established in German-occupied Poland.

28 September: Poland capitulates.

1940

January: Mass shootings of Jews carried out.

25 January: A new German concentration camp is established at the Polish town of Oswiecim – Auschwitz.

April–May: The NKVD massacres 26,000 Polish officers at Katyn Forest near Smolensk.

30 April: The first Jewish ghetto is sealed off in Łódź, Poland, entrapping 230,000 Jews.

14 June: Paris falls to the Germans.

10 August: Anti-Jewish laws promulgated in Romania.

23 September: Himmler sets up a special SS bank account, under the name 'Max Heiliger', for deposits of gold (including from teeth), silver, jewellery and currency taken from murdered or incarcerated Jews.

October: Jews are compelled to pay and erect a wall around their own ghetto in Warsaw.

20–24 November: Hungary, Romania, and Slovakia join the Axis powers.

1941

25 March: Yugoslavia joins the Axis.

May: Personnel for the Einsatzgruppen and Einsatzkommandos are recruited, organized and prepared for the occupation of the Balkans, the Soviet Union and for Operation Sea Lion, the invasion of Britain.

22 June: Operation Barbarossa sees the Nazi invasion of the Soviet Union. In the Soviet village of Virbalis, Einsatzgruppen machine-gun all adult Jews.

2 July: Heydrich instructs the Einsatzgruppen and Kommandos participating in Operation Barbarossa to execute communist office holders, Jews in state employment, and other 'radical elements'.

15 July: Smolensk is captured by German troops.

31 July: Hermann Göring authorizes Heydrich to implement *Endlösung der Judenfrage* – the Final Solution in all German-held territories.

August: Tens of thousands of Jews are murdered throughout the western Soviet Union, Lithuania, Romania and Latvia, the majority by Einsatzgruppen squads.

September: The use of explosives and motor-vehicle exhaust fumes to kill large numbers of people are tested on asylum patients at the Novinki and Mogilev asylums near Minsk; Kiev, capital of the Ukraine, falls to the German army.

27 September: Heydrich is appointed Deputy Reich Protector of the Protectorate of Bohemia and Moravia, and moves to Prague.

10 October: Heydrich chairs a meeting of the RHSA in Prague to finalize plans for the deportation of 50,000 Jews in the territory to ghettos in Minsk and Riga.

29–30 September: The Babi Yar massacre of Jews in Kiev, in which 34,000 men, women and children are murdered.

12 October: Heydrich disseminates Report No. 111, stating: 'The principal targets of execution by the Einsatzkommandos will be: political functionaries ... Jews mistakenly released from POW camps ... Jewish sadists and avengers ... Jews in general'.

December: The widespread murder of Jews in the east continues; Einsatzkommando 3 reports killing over 136,000 Jews since June 1941.

16 December: Governor-General of German-occupied Poland, Hans Frank, notes that there are 3,500,000 Jews resident in his region.

1942

20 January: Top Nazi and SS officers meet in Wannsee, Berlin, to coordinate the final solution to the Jewish question.

May: Heydrich orders the obliteration of evidence of Einsatzgruppen massacres in the east.

4 June: Heydrich dies of sepsis from wounds sustained in an assassination attempt in Prague on 27 May; in reprisal, all males over the age of 16 in the villages of Lidice and Ležáky are executed.

1943

30 January: SS-Obergruppenführer Ernst Kaltenbrunner succeeds Heydrich as head of the RHSA.

1944

May: The incineration of bodies massacred by the Einsatzgruppen to destroy evidence commences.

20 July: Senior German army officers fail in their attempt to assassinate Hitler.

1945

30 April: Adolf Hitler commits suicide in his Berlin bunker.

6 May: Grand Admiral Karl Dönitz, Hitler's successor, strips Himmler of all his positions.

8 May: Nazi Germany surrenders, ending the war in Europe.

12 May: Ernst Kaltenbrunner is arrested.

21 May: Heinrich Himmler is arrested.

23 May: Himmler commits suicide.

Otto Adolf Eichmann, the leading architect of the 'deportation' of Eastern European Jews to extermination camps in Nazi-occupied territories, in the yard of Ayalon Prison in Israel, 1961. (Photo GPO, Israel)

INTRODUCTION

My dearest,
Before I die, I am writing a few words,
We are about to die, five thousand innocent people,
They are cruelly shooting us,
Kisses to you all,
Mira ...

> Translation of a Yiddish note, found in a woman's clothing, during
> an exhumation carried out in October 1944 at the murder
> site of Jews near the village of Antanase, Lithuania.
> Source: Yad Vashem.

From the mid-1300s, Jews had begun to settle in a large tract of Eastern European territory known as the 'Pale of the Settlement'. By 1900, there were an estimated 7 million Jews living in an area bounded by Germany on the west, the Baltic Sea on the north, the Black Sea on the south and the Dnieper River in Russia on the east. The Jewish population of Poland in 1939 was about 3.3 million, while an additional 2.1 million resided in the occupied Soviet provinces.

In September 1939, the Sicherheitsdienst (Security Service, or SD) and the Sicherheitspolizei (Security Police, or SiPo) were merged to become the Reichssicherheitshauptamt (Reich Main Security Office, or RSHA), headed by the Chef der Sicherheitspolizei und des Sicherheitsdienst (Chief of Security Police and SD, or CSSD).

The mass murder of 'racially impure' individuals began with the German invasion of the Soviet Union on 22 June 1941. By the end of the year, some 80 per cent of Lithuanian Jews had been massacred, and by the beginning of 1943, most of the Jews of the western parts of Ukraine and Belorussia had been annihilated. Additionally, Romanians and Germans murdered 150,000 Romanian and Ukrainian Jews in the first months after the invasion of the Soviet Union.

In January 1942, a conference was held in Wannsee, a suburb of Berlin, in order to coordinate the implementation of the 'Final Solution of the Jewish Question', the codename for the plan to murder all Jews within German-occupied territories.

The catalyst in the Nazis' plan to solve the Jewish problem was triggered with Operation Barbarossa, the large-scale German invasion of the Soviet Union. The massive military offensive, scheduled to be over by winter, had been planned for a considerably long time. In anticipation, the Germans had raised units of Ukrainian, Lithuanian, Latvian and Belorussian nationalist and oppositionist collaborators to assist with achieving the objective.

Hitler considered the invasion of the Soviet Union as part of his plan to provide the Fatherland with *lebensraum,* or living space, while providing an opportunity to destroy the Bolsheviks and communism he so despised.

In the first weeks of Barbarossa, Jewish women and children were only shot when they 'got in the way', but by the middle of August, the parameters of the pogrom had been extended to include all Jews, regardless of gender or age.

Pursuant to Hitler's desire for a more structured and efficient resolution to the Jewish problem, four special action groups – Einsatzgruppen – paved the way for the systematic mass murder of the Jews. The battalion-sized groups comprised SS, police and Eastern European auxiliaries recruited from the local population.

Hundreds of thousands of Jews managed to flee into the vastness of the Soviet Union, but millions were trapped under Nazi occupation. Over a million would become the innocent and defenceless victims of mass murder carried out by the Einsatzgruppen units. In the six months to the end of 1941, around half a million Jews were murdered in a swathe stretching from the Baltic States in the north, through Belorussia, and to the Ukraine on the shores of the Black Sea in the south.

The murders generally took place in secluded spots such as in forests, valleys and ravines close to the homes of the victims, where they were forced to divest themselves of all clothing and valuables a short distance from the pits where they would be shot and buried – Babi Yar, Kiev, Lidice, Minsk, Riga, the Ponar, Blagovshchina and Rumbula forests, Trostinets, Drobytsky Yar, Simferopol, Kharkov, Kaunas, Kovno, Vilnius, Łódź ...

Estimates still vary as historians and scholars debate the accuracy of numbers of Jews exterminated by the Einsatzgruppen, but it is generally accepted that, of the six million Jewish victims of the Holocaust, the shooting operations and gas wagons of the mobile killing squads at hundreds of locations in German-occupied Eastern Europe accounted

Waffen-SS SS-Obersturmführer wearing the Totenkopf collar badge. (Photo Bundesarchiv)

Judenstern. (Photo JMW)

for at least 1.3 million Jews, in addition to tens of thousands of Soviet Communist officials, partisans and gypsies.

In his diary, Hitler's propaganda chief, Joseph Goebbels not only summed up the Nazis' 'Final Solution' agenda, but also the mechanism and manner in which this would be achieved – initially the role of the specially selected and appointed Einsatzgruppen death squads: 'The Führer once again expressed his determination to clean up the Jews in Europe pitilessly. There must be no squeamish sentimentalism about it. The Jews have deserved the catastrophe that has now overtaken them. Their destruction will go hand in hand with the destruction of our enemies. We must hasten this process with cold ruthlessness.

'The procedure is a pretty barbaric one and not to be described here more definitely. Not much will remain of the Jews. On the whole it can be said that about 60 per cent of them will have to be liquidated whereas only 40 per cent can be used for forced labour.'

1. MY LOYALTY IS MY HONOUR

BLACKEST PAGE IN HISTORY

23 Nazi Officers Face Trial

Twenty-three former commanding officers of the 'S.S. Einsatzgruppen' – special task commandos – who are being charged with killing more than 1,000,000 Jews, gypsies and other anti-Nazis, were described by the prosecution in Nuremberg yesterday as 'cruel executioners whose terror has written the blackest page in human history.'

Mr Benjamin Ferencz, leading the U.S. prosecution, said of them: 'Death was their tool and life their toy.

'If these men be immune, then law has lost its meaning and men must live in fear.'

The men accused of this 'world's biggest murder case,' who pleaded not guilty at a previous formal sitting, were alleged to have established a ghastly record of wild butchery, killing on an average fifty persons an hour over two years.

It is expected that the trial will only take three days. The opening speech was the shortest at any of the eight trials held by the Americans since the first international war criminals' trial.

Aberdeen Press and Journal, Tuesday, 30 September 1947

The dogmatic and zealous fundamental belief in the superiority of the German people – specifically the Aryan race – is not unique to the Nazi faithful of the Second World War.

Regarded as the first ethnic genocide of the twentieth century, from 1904 to 1907, as many as 65,000 men, women and children of the indigenous Herero and Nama tribes, perished at the hands of their colonial masters in German South West Africa (Namibia). Despite a 'protection' treaty entered into by the Herero and Imperial Germany's colonial governor and father to Luftwaffe commander Hermann Göring, Heinrich Göring, German settlers confiscated Herero land and livestock, while using the tribespeople as slaves.

When the Herero rose in rebellion, Berlin despatched a force of 14,000 Schutztruppe (colonial protection troops) under Prussian officer Lieutenant General Lothar von Trotha to the colony to suppress the insurrection. On his arrival on 11 June 1904, von Trotha declared his plan to resolve the

Prussian officer General Lothar von Trotha is met by fellow officers in German South West Africa.

Herero issue: 'I believe that the nation as such should be annihilated, or, if this was not possible by tactical measures, have to be expelled from the country.'

After defeating a 'force' of Hereros at Waterberg, the Schutztruppe shot and bayoneted to death every Herero they could find, regardless of age or gender. On 2 October, von Trotha issued a proclamation declaring that the Herero were no longer German subjects, and were therefore required to leave the country. His troops were ordered to kill every male Herero they encountered, but to maintain the 'good reputation of the German soldier', they were to drive all women and children into the desert to die of thirst and starvation. Trotha added that the rebellion 'is and remains the beginning of a racial struggle'.

Whilst fully agreeing with von Trotha's definition of the conflict as being racial, Chief of the Imperial German General Staff, Generalfeldmarschall Alfred von Schlieffen, did not approve of the methodology. As a consequence, from the end of 1904, the Herero were incarcerated in concentration camps, such as Shark Island, and employed as slave labour under horrific conditions. Starvation and disease claimed the lives of thousands. In a chilling prelude to a common Nazi practice, inhuman medical experiments were performed on prisoners, and as many as 300 skulls were shipped to Berlin for research and experimentation.

Unwittingly, the Herero experience would provide a historical template for Hitler's Holocaust, perhaps drawing inspiration from something von Trotha

THE HERERO RISING

Treatment of Natives
(Reuter's Telegram) Berlin, Tuesday: Increasing light has been thrown on the cause of the Herero rising in South-West Africa. Nettled by the attacks made on the missionaries the 'Reichsbote,' the official organ of German Protestantism, now accuses the German settlers in the colony of having driven the Hereros to desperation by their brutalities and usury, their general methods of trade, as well as by their expropriation of native property.

The Journal declares that the Germans are accustomed to flog the natives with sticks and rhinoceros hides whips, 25 strokes being often inflicted on innocent blacks. It mentions cases of natives swooning under such punishment, and falling in a pool of blood.

The 'Reichsbote' maintains that the Hereros were formerly peaceful people, whereas now, in consequence of the behaviour of the whites, they have become filled with intense hatred of the Germans. Finally, the 'Reichsbote' repudiates the charge that the Hereros are slaying women and children alike; on the contrary, it declares that the Hereros have spared the German women and children, and concludes by asserting that they were driven to rebellion, as the whites respected neither native women nor native property.

The 'Kreuz Zeitung' [Prussian conservative newspaper taken over by the Nazi Party in August 1937] expresses a hope that the methods of the Conquistadores in Mexico will not be imitated by the German soldiers in suppressing the rising. It demands that every case of shooting unarmed natives or prisoners shall meet with exemplary punishment.

The colonial organs demand more rigorous measures against the natives and stronger reinforcements.

Western Daily Press, Wednesday, 23 March 1904

once wrote: 'I destroy the African tribes with streams of blood ... Only following this cleansing can something new emerge, which will remain.'

On 22 June 1941, the Soviet Union was attacked on a broad front by three German armies as Hitler launched Operation Barbarossa. Tearing up the fraudulent pact with which Hitler had duped Stalin to buy him time to adequately subjugate Western Europe, this was no ordinary war. Fuelled by patriotic propaganda, the Führer demanded absolute loyalty and pride for his war of annihilation to succeed. The Bolsheviks were the dregs of humanity, and, together with the Jews, had to be removed from the face of the earth to provide his master race with *lebensraum*, that extra room in which to expand and flourish. His war machine was duty bound to destroy and not to just conquer his most-hated enemy to the east, zealously spurred on: 'The German soldier has now proved his valour, saving Europe from Bolshevism, enemy of the world.'

Hitler's master plan to cleanse Eastern Europe required a disciplined and ruthless individual whose fervent loyalty to the Reich was beyond question and his integrity impeccable.

The 41-year-old SS-Reichsführer Heinrich Himmler was the perfect choice. Chief of the German Police, Reich Commissar for the Consolidation of the Ethnic German Nation, Reich Minister of the Interior, and Commander of the Reserve Army, Himmler *was* the Schutzstaffel (SS). He lived the National Socialist ideology, and as his Führer's security-measures envoy, he would compose and orchestrate the grand design for the 'Aryanization' of an ethnically sullied Eastern Europe through the instrument of racial selection and genocide.

Born on 7 October 1900, the son of a well-placed Munich schoolteacher, Heinrich Himmler grew up in a regulated home environment, characterized by a robust work ethic combined with strict religious obedience. The royalist, conservative and financially comfortable Himmler family shunned the liberal modernity of Munich in the early 1900s. With the birth in December 1905 of younger brother Ernst, Heinrich was now the middle child, junior to brother Gebhard. Heinrich suddenly found himself confronting significantly diluted parental attention.

SS-Reichsführer Heinrich Himmler (centre) with SS-Obergruppenführer August Eigruber visit Mauthausen concentration camp, east of Linz, Upper Austria.

16

Although small in stature, the frail and illness-prone Heinrich evolved into an individualist, determined to define his own future, as witnessed by his entries into a diary that he maintained religiously. Only 14 years old at the outbreak of the Great War, Himmler watched with great envy as his 17-year-old brother, Gebhard, enlisted in the army reserve. Writing, 'If only I were old enough,' the besotted Himmler would spend hours with his friends playing war games. His diary accounts, however, often read like real conflict as he 'fought' the enemies of Germany and Austria.

From April 1915, Himmler enlisted for the summer with the Jugendwehr, or Cadet Corps, where he received his first taste of the basics of military training. He continued with this pre-military training in the Landshut Cadet Corps, in the town where his father was now a teaching professor. In 1917, and despite connections in the Bavarian royal family, Himmler's father failed to have his son accepted for officer training in one of the Bavarian regiments. This setback, though hugely disappointing, did not hinder the teenager's aspirations of becoming an officer in an elite German regiment. In October, the Regensburg city administration accepted his application to join the patriotic auxiliary service's welfare office. With the threat of conscription – which would have dashed his hopes for officer training – Himmler returned to grammar school, but not for long.

On 23 December, the ecstatic Himmler received notification that he had been accepted as a candidate for officer training in the 11th Infantry Regiment, based near Regensburg. However, this had a major impact on Himmler – he became extremely homesick. His only consolation, albeit slight, were the letters from home. If, after just a few days he had not heard from his mother, the fractious Himmler would admonish his parents for failing in their duties to look after his welfare. His craving for parental affection and attention was insatiable, and he did all he could to get home at every available weekend.

The Armistice on November 1918 and the capitulation of Germany left Himmler inconsolably devastated. Unlike his brother Gebhard (who had earned the Iron Cross), Himmler did not see action, which, for him, was an abject failure. The final humiliation came with his discharge on 18 December, his dreams of fulfilling his true vocation in shreds.

In the months that followed, Himmler wrote his school-leavers examination (*Abitur*) and joined the Bavarian People's Party (BPP).

For Heinrich Himmler, 1919 was a seminal year that would lay the foundation for the ruthless SS officer of the future. In that year, he made the unlikely decision to study agriculture at the Technical University in Munich. Physically, the young Himmler remained prone to illness, and in September, was diagnosed with an enlarged heart. During periods of hospitalization, Himmler became a

GERMAN PLOT

Ludendorff and His Party the Real Danger
Speaking in the Prussian Diet, on Saturday, Herr Severing, the Minister of the Interior, referred to General Ludendorff and to Rossbach and Hitler as constituting the most dangerous elements in the conspiracy against the Republic. These persons, he said, form the German "Folk" or anti-Semitic Party in the Reichstag. They are in close collaboration with Count Reventlow, whose name, however, has not so far been publicly mentioned in connection with the affair.

The excitement following Herr Severing's exposure in the Reichstag of a Nationalist plot against the State has, says the Central News, by no means subsided, and Berlin is full of alarmist reports. The Nationalists have refused to obey the Prussian decrees ordering them to dissolve, and Herr Adolf Hitler is said to be mobilising his Fascisti for an immediate march on Berlin. The police have been doubled in strength round the principal buildings, and extensive precautions have been taken. Numerous arrests were made on Saturday in Thuringian towns.

Sheffield Daily Telegraph, Monday, 26 March 1923

prolific reader of books, with a particular penchant for historical fiction. Towards the end of this medical interlude, Himmler read the popular discourse on the evils of Freemasonry by contentious writer Friedrich Wichtl, *Weltfreimaurerei – Weltrevolution – Weltrepublik* (Freemasonry – World revolution – World republic). The controversial work laid the blame for the disastrous and humiliating First World War defeat squarely at the feet of international Freemasonry. In their activities, as they strove toward a world revolution, the Freemasons were powerfully influenced by Jews. The seed was planted.

A practising Catholic who regularly attended mass and communion, Himmler started identifying with anti-Semitic German nationalism, placing him in conflict with his deep-rooted religious beliefs. Bizarrely, Himmler indicated in his diary that 'God will show me the way in all my doubts' – he had placated his inner conflict between the Church and anti-Semitism.

In 1922, his agricultural studies reaching a conclusion, Himmler entered a phase of nationalist political enlightenment as the hated Weimar Republic, which sacrificed German honour by signing the surrender at Versailles, polarized the German nation. Increasingly, Right-wing activism attracted members of the German *volk* disillusioned with the prevailing instability. This was a period of foundation radicalization for Himmler, his graduation with a diploma in agriculture marking the end of the chapter of his formative years that were punctuated with profound insecurity.

In response to the sway the Communist Party of Germany (KPD) held over the socialist governments of Saxony and Thuringia, the Sturmabteilung (SA) of the Nazi Party – the infamous 'brown shirts' – formed the Deutsche Kampfbund, or German Combat League.

After the failed pro-Hitler putsch in November 1923, in which the armed and uniformed Himmler was the flag bearer of the *Reichskriegsflagge* (war ensign), he developed a growing interest in leading Nazi activist Adolf Hitler. Himmler now became a fulltime fighter for the cause, speaking at meetings in Lower Bavaria, Westphalia and in the cities of northern Germany. His speeches increasingly came to be dominated by talk of the dangerous threat posed by Jews and Bolsheviks – the latter a euphemism for communists. 'Party comrade Himmler' was in demand for his public oration.

In 1926, Himmler joined the staff at party headquarters in Munich, where, as deputy Reich propaganda chief, he organized the rigid intra-party reporting system that became synonymous with the Third Reich of the Second World War. In November 1927, his reward for flawlessly arranging public addresses by party leaders came in the form of a promotion to Deputy SS-Reichsführer.

Formed in 1925, the SS – Schutzstaffel – was responsible for providing protection for party leaders and at party meetings; it was made up of notorious, feared and strongly built skull-bashers. Himmler rapidly developed an intelligence framework within the SS: the eyes and ears of the party on the ground. He further introduced SS-specific military drills and uniforms.

The *totenkopf*, or death's head skull and crossbones symbol, has its origins as a military symbol in the reign of eighteenth-century Prussian king, Frederick the Great. Seen here on an SA standard in Braunschweig, 1932. (Photo Bundesarchiv)

THE TOLL OF DACHAU

Many unemployed are sent to Germany and they don't like it. In the working-class districts of Vienna and along the high road to the South, one could notice the inscriptions, "We would rather have Schuschnigg back, we are fed up with Hitler." Businessmen, hard hit by the collapse of the Jews, are struggling against a flood of new regulations, restrictions and innumerable forms to be filled out. The strict control of every business activity increases the apprehension of the middle-class that arbitrary expropriation will not stop at the Jews.

The Nazi authorities are well aware of the growing restlessness. They increase terror to satisfy their needy followers. They were disappointed to get only £20 million out of the Jews. To prevent any movement of resistance numerous arrests have been made, judges, generals, and high civil servants among them. "It seems that every patriotic Austrian is being sent to Dachau," a former official said. Dachau, the notorious concentration camp, takes its terrible toll. Every week sealed coffins or urns are sent to Austria. Schuschnigg is said to be working there on the moors. Outstanding men of the former regime like Colonel Adam and Burgomaster Schmitz, have met their dreadful end there. Others are known to have lost an eye or an arm. There are 60,000 political prisoners in Austria, 20,000 Jews among them – 10 per cent of the entire Jewish population.

Nazi rule in Austria means the exploitation of the country for German armaments, mass terror, and a kind of mob-Communism, up to now directed mainly against the Jews. The conviction that "This cannot last" is spreading again among the people, Nazis and non-Nazis, and many are realising for the first time that Austrians are different from the Germans. But for the time being the "spider flag," as the Swastika is called by the peasants, seems be firmly entrenched in Austria.

Yorkshire Post and Leeds Intelligencer, Thursday, 23 June 1938

In January 1927, Hitler appointed Himmler as SS-Reichsführer, replacing Erhard Heiden in a move clouded with intrigue. Six years later, on orders from Himmler and his chief lieutenant, Reinhard Heydrich, Heiden was arrested and murdered.

Himmler introduced his 'Engagement and Marriage Order' in 1931, to ensure that the racial integrity of members of the SS remained 'of strictly Nordic origin', intended wives had to be vetted by the new Racial Office.

Himmler continued to display his meticulous organizational capabilities, creating SS *Abschnitt*, or district, brigade structures, to which he appointed commanders generally born from 1890 to 1900, who had a tertiary education, and who had served in the First World War. From this carefully selected pool of leaders, would emerge the names of some of the most notorious Nazi mass murderers of the Second World War.

Himmler's additional appointment as Bavarian Political Police Commander coincided with the creation in March 1933 of the SS camp at Dachau, the model for all future concentration and extermination camps. Initially constructed at the site of an old gunpowder factory at Dachau near Munich to house prisoners in 'protective custody', on 11 April the SS took over the camp together with its 200 inhabitants. Unprecedented brutality against the prisoners commenced immediately, with gross maltreatment and executions. This drew immediate condemnation from the Bavarian justice and interior ministers, who called on Himmler to replace the camp commandant, Hilmar Wäckerle. Himmler could not have been more pleased with this unexpected development, as he now had free licence to install his own man as commander of the soon-to-be death camp: SS-Brigadeführer Theodor Eicke.

A loyal Nazi, Eicke soon became chief of the Concentration Camps Inspectorate, followed by his appointment in 1936 as commander of the SS-Totenkopfverbände (Death's Head Troops). Eicke gained infamy as head of the SS-Totenkopf Division during Operation Barbarossa.

Speaking at the Prussian Interior Ministry on assuming the role of chief of the German police, Himmler declared that the expanded national police force was necessary to fulfil the role of protection of the state against internal and external threats and enemies:

We are in a country in the heart of Europe surrounded by open borders, surrounded by a world that is becoming more and more Bolshevized, and increasingly taken over by the Jew in his worst form, namely the tyranny of a totally destructive Bolshevism. To believe that this development is going to come to an end in a year's time, or in several years or even decades, is culpably reckless and erroneous.

We must assume that this struggle will last for generations, for it's the age-old struggle between humans and subhumans in its current new phase of the struggle between the Aryan peoples and Jewry and the organizational form

Jewry has adopted of Bolshevism. I see my task as being to prepare the whole nation for this struggle by building up the police welded together with the order of the SS as the organization to protect the Reich at home just as the Wehrmacht provides protection against threats from abroad.

From *Heinrich Himmler*, Peter Longerich, Oxford University Press, 2012

In mid-1931, Himmler made a key decision in the history of the SS: the establishment of an independent SS intelligence service, headed up by former naval *nachrichtenoffizier*, (information officer) Reinhard Heydrich.

Born on 7 March 1904 of wealthy parents, Reinhard Heydrich had a strict childhood in the mould of patriotic German nationalism. In 1919, the 15-year-old Heydrich enlisted with Maercker's Volunteer Rifles – the first *freikorps* – during the civil unrest between communists and non-communists in his home town of Halle. The events had a significant impact on his developing political thinking, and proved to be the catalyst for his joining the anti-Semitic Deutschvölkischer Schutz und Trutzbund (National German Protection and Shelter League).

SS-Obergruppenführer und General der Polizei Reinhard Tristan Eugen Heydrich. (Photo Bundesarchiv)

In 1922, Heydrich enrolled in the Reichsmarine as a naval cadet in the German navy, receiving his commission in 1926. However, the status of rank fuelled arrogance in the young sub-lieutenant, leading to a reputation as a womanizer. In 1931, he was cashiered from the navy for getting his fiancée pregnant and then failing in his duty to marry her. He then became a devoted servant of the Nazi Party, and, in that same year, he was interviewed by Himmler in Munich to head the new SS counterintelligence section.

The following year, the ambitious Heydrich was appointed chief of the retitled security service: the Sicherheitsdienst (SD). On 22 April 1934, Himmler made Heydrich head of the Gestapo, the Prussian police force formed by Hermann Göring in 1933.

The 'Night of the Long Knives' was the name given to Hitler's three-day purge of the party which started on the night of 30 June 1934. At the Führer's behest, Heydrich, Himmler, Göring, and future SA chief, Viktor Lutze, compiled lists of those to be 'removed', starting with the seven top SA officials. Heydrich's erstwhile mentor and current SA chief, Ernst Röhm, was one of 200 unceremoniously shot without trial during the witch hunt. At the execution of Gregor Strasser, deemed a political enemy, the bullet missed the vital nerve and Strasser lay bleeding from the neck. Heydrich's voice was heard from the corridor: 'Not dead yet? Let the swine bleed to death.'

In 1936, Heydrich became chief of the Sicherheitspolizei (Security Police, or SiPo), which included the criminal police, the security service, and the Gestapo. With the SA neutered into a sports and training organization, Heydrich had a totally clear field. The Gestapo Law was

Poster identifying the Ordnungspolizei, (national uniformed police) and the Sicherheitspolizei (Security Police), early recruitment pools for the Einsatzgruppen. (Photo Bundesarchiv)

promulgated in 1936, giving the Nazi organ, whose very name engendered fear and terror, carte blanche to exercise *schutzhaft* – 'protective custody'. The definition of an alleged crime was entirely at the Gestapo's discretion, allowing for arbitrary powers of arrest and incarceration without judicial formalities.

In 1938, Heydrich formulated the idea of the Einsatzgruppen, whose sole business would be to murder Jews and other 'enemies of the Reich'. The results were unimaginable. In two years, the 3,000 operatives of these 'action groups' slaughtered at least a million people. In November of that year, he waded into an event that in some way not only provided concrete evidence of his barbarity, but also presaged his own death. Herschel Grynszpan, the teenage son of a Polish Jew whom he had deported from Germany, shot German diplomat Ernst von Rath in Paris on 7 November. Von Rath succumbed to his wounds two days later. In reprisal Heydrich ordered the pogrom *Kristallnacht* (Crystal Night). On the night of 9 November, throughout Germany, some 200 synagogues, many Jewish cemeteries, more than 7,000 Jewish shops and 29 department stores were damaged,

FUNERAL OF VON RATH

Hitler's Unwonted Silence

BITTER SORROW

Obsequies Like Those for a King

Herr Hitler was strangely silent at Dusseldorf yesterday at the funeral of Herr von Rath, the German Embassy Secretary who was shot in Paris by a 17-year-old Polish Jew. A violent anti-Jewish speech by the Fuehrer had been expected.

The stage was set for such an utterance. Chiefs of the Government and Nazi Party were with Hitler in Rhine Hall, where the body had lain in state all night. The ceremony was such that the obsequies might have been those of a king.

VEHEMENT OUTBURSTS

But Hitler said nothing. The only speeches were made by State Secretary Bohle, leader of the Nazi organisation of Germans Abroad, and Herr von Ribbentrop, Foreign Minister and formerly Ambassador in London. The Fuehrer, who had stood bowed in reverence before the catafalque during a Beethoven funeral march, listened, shook hands with von Rath's family, saluted the coffin and left the hall. Herr Bohle, who was educated in South Africa during the war, said: "My leader, once more the whole German nation stand bitterly and in deep sorrow before the bier of one more German forced to sacrifice his life on foreign soil for that Germany which he has so faithfully served." After referring to the murder in Davos, Switzerland, of the Nazi leader Wilhelm Gustloff, and to Nazis who died in Spain, Herr Bohle declared: The shots tired in Davos, Spain, and Paris, have had only one target. That target is Germany.

"Germans all over the world are pursuing their labours as loyal guests of the State. They are living there to-day – the objects of hatred, persecution and slander by the international submen who are concentrating all their powers at destroying the restored Reich. The Reich, which has been saved from within and without by Adolf Hitler, will give these elements no longer any opportunity to continue their sinister work against Germany from within. The Jews, according to their own admission, have wanted to harm Germany, and we are able to confirm that Germany has been very seriously harmed. The Jews, however, overlook one thing – namely, that dead National Socialists never weaken the movement which has made Germany once more a world Power, but that they are more determined to be victorious."

JEWRY'S "WEAPONS"

Herr von Ribbentrop said: "We stand in mourning before our great colleague Von Rath, who has been killed by the bullet of the Jewish murderer. The entire German people are in mourning, and a hostile world believes that they are able to delay the advance of our fate through blind hatred. Terror and murder are the weapons of international Jewry. The old world is sinking. No terror can bring back the slavery of Germany. What the future may bring we do not know, but Germany will stand strong and united as never before. Never will a people go under which has men who are willing to die in order that the people may live. If new hatred meets us in the world to-day, then a storm of indignation will run through the German people. Conscious of its strength, the people stand united behind its leader, and all march with him towards the great German future." – Reuter.

Northern Whig, Friday, 18 November 1938

and in many cases destroyed, and houses ransacked. More than 30,000 Jewish men were arrested and taken to concentration camps, mainly at Dachau, Buchenwald and Sachsenhausen.

In 1939, SiPo merged with the RSHA, with Heydrich as its leader. In this role, he orchestrated the 31 August Polish 'attack' on Gleiwitz (today in Poland), an important element in the stage-setting for the invasion of Poland the next day. In an operation known as '*Grossmutter gestorben*' (grandmother died), Germans in Polish uniforms staged an 'attack' on the local radio station – ostensibly the work of anti-German Polish saboteurs. Heydrich arranged for a dozen prisoners from Dachau concentration camp to be dressed in Polish uniforms, then drugged and shot and their bodies dumped at the 'battlefield'. It was likely Heydrich who chose the code phrase '*konserve*' (canned goods) for these first casualties of the Second World War.

Heinrich (centre) and Obergruppenführer Karl Hermann Frank (right) in Prague. Frank would organize the massacre of the people of Lidice. (Photo Bundesarchiv)

At this time, Bohemia and Moravia had already been elevated from independent status to that of *Reichsprotektorat*, with Baron Konstantin von Neurath, Hitler's aged former foreign minister, designated Protector of the Czechs. However, despite his achievements in abolishing Czech political parties and trade unions, instituting the Nürnberg racial laws in the protectorate, and making Czechoslovakian industry work for the German war effort, he was accused of being 'too lenient'.

On 3 September 1941, von Neurath was replaced by SS-Obergruppenführer Heydrich. The German icon moved into the old royal palace in Hradčany, Prague. The executions started – 300 in the first five weeks. His requiem for Gregor Strasser became his dirge for all patriotic Czechs: 'Aren't they dead yet? Let them bleed to death.'

Heydrich had come a long way in his life of thirty-eight years. He had stood trial three times because of Nazi Party doubts about the purity of his Aryan pedigree. Now, as chief of the RSHA, which he continued to run from Czechoslovakia, he was executioner to all of occupied Europe. Heydrich wielded immense power, so much so that he could force chief of the Abwehr (German intelligence), Admiral Wilhelm Canaris, to travel to Prague where, at the end of May 1942, he was obliged to sign away the independence of the Abwehr and accept subordination to the SD. It was his moment of greatest personal triumph. A few days later he was dead. Heydrich died on 4 June of sepsis developed from multiple wounds sustained during an assassination attempt on 27 May.

At an elaborate ceremony befitting that of a head of state, Himmler pronounced the funeral oration, calling him 'that good and radiant man'. Personally attending, Hitler placed Heydrich's decorations on his funeral pillow, including the highest grade of the German Order, the Blood Order Medal, the Wound Badge in Gold, and the War Merit Cross, 1st Class with Swords. The Czechs would pay dearly for Heydrich's death.

The Einsatzgruppen death-squad concept, as the instrument to implement mass-murder cleansing pogroms, was first introduced in Operation Tannenberg

(*Unternehmen Tannenberg*), the extermination of Polish citizens whose nation had been swallowed by Hitler's blitzkrieg in September 1939:

Chief of Security Police and SD, or CSSD
SS-Obergruppenführer und General der Polizei Reinhard Tristan Eugen Heydrich

Einsatzgruppe I – Wien (Fourteenth Army)
Commanding Officer SS-Standartenführer Bruno Streckenbach
Einsatzkommando 1/I: SS-Sturmbannführer Ludwig Hahn
Einsatzkommando 2/I: SS-Sturmbannführer Bruno Müller
Einsatzkommando 3/I: SS-Sturmbannführer Alfred Hasselberg
Einsatzkommando 4/I: SS-Sturmbannführer Karl Brunner

Einsatzgruppe II – Oppeln (Tenth Army)
Commanding Officer SS-Obersturmbannführer Emanuel Schäfer
Einsatzkommando 1/II: SS-Obersturmbannführer Otto Sens
Einsatzkommando 2/II: SS-Sturmbannführer Karl-Heinz Rux

Einsatzgruppe III – Breslau (Eighth Army)
Commanding Officer SS-Obersturmbannführer Hans Fischer
Einsatzkommando 1/III: SS-Sturmbannführer Wilhelm Scharpwinkel
Einsatzkommando 2/III: SS-Sturmbannführer Fritz Liphardt

Einsatzgruppe IV – Dramburg (Fourth Army)
Commanding Officer SS-Brigadeführer Lothar Beutel and Standartenführer
    Josef Albert 'Butcher of Warsaw' Meisinger in 1939
Einsatzkommando 1/IV: SS-Sturmbannführer Helmut Bischoff
Einsatzkommando 2/IV: SS-Sturmbannführer Walter Hammer

Einsatzgruppe V – Allenstein (Third Army)
Commanding Officer SS-Standartenführer Ernst Damzog
Einsatzkommando 1/V: SS-Sturmbannführer Heinz Gräfe
Einsatzkommando 2/V: SS-Sturmbannführer Robert Schefe
Einsatzkommando 3/V: SS-Sturmbannführer Walter Albath

Einsatzgruppe VI (Wielkopolska area)
Commanding Officer SS-Oberführer Erich Naumann
Einsatzkommando 1/VI: SS-Sturmbannführer Franz Sommer
Einsatzkommando 2/VI: SS-Sturmbannführer Gerhard Flesch

Einsatzgruppe z. B.V. (Upper Silesia and Cieszyn Silesia areas)
Commanding Officer SS-Obergruppenführer Udo von Woyrsch and
SS-Oberführer Otto Rasch

Einsatzkommando 16 – Danzig (Pomorze area)
Commanding Officer SS-Sturmbannführer Rudolf Tröger

The 3,000-strong Einsatzgruppen (task forces) were hastily reformed and trained
by the Sicherheitshauptamt (Head Security Office) of Reinhard Heydrich, ready
to follow in the wake of the conquering Eastern Front Wehrmacht.

The brigade was divided into four battalion-sized units – A, B, C and D – each
responsible for the four large territorial theatres of invasion and occupation.
Each Einsatzgruppen comprised Einsatzkommandos and/or Sonderkommandos,
not unlike companies in a battalion.

While the battalions were largely made up of former police officers from low-
er-class backgrounds, the various *gruppen* and *kommando* commanders throughout
the structure were carefully selected: mintellectuals were sought and appointed, not

A unit of the SS Totenkopf
Division crosses into the
Soviet Union in 1941.
(Photo Bundesarchiv)

BERCHTESGADEN LEGEND

The greatest of the German Emperors was Frederick Barbarossa. He is one of Germany's national heroes. In concluding his chapter on Barbarossa, Bryce tells of the legend that Barbarossa and his knights lie in an enchanted sleep in a cavern near Berchtesgaden, waiting there until summoned to come to Germany's aid when he will bring back again to Germany peace and strength and unity.

It is Berchtesgaden Hitler has chosen for his home. Is that a bit of stage management, for which he is famous? Is it meant to recall the old legend and to suggest that he is the Barbarossa of the century, destined to recover for Germany all the power and prestige it enjoyed when its king was also the head off the Holy Roman Empire? He is already – as a glance at the map of Europe will show – master of a greater empire than either Charlemagne or Barbarossa possessed. But there is one difference between Hitler and the German hero whom, perhaps, he is imitating. Barbarossa, according to his lights, was a believing man. He was zealous of his Christian allegiance. He died in Asia when leading the third crusade against the Saracens.

Hitler, on the other hand, stands for a revived paganism. He represents a reversion to sheer barbarism. He has won his empire, such as it is, by trickery, deception, treachery and lying – methods which Charlemagne and Barbarossa would have scorned to use. And he maintains it by cruelty and terrorism and massacre. It is a Holy Roman Empire no longer. It represents the home of power and darkness.

Here, then, are the two empires – Mussolini's dream of the ancient secular Roman Empire; Hitler's dream of a revived Holy Roman Empire with Germany as the dominant nation. At present the two dictators seem to be working amicably together, though Mussolini is already reduced to the position of being Hitler's lackey. But it is inevitable that the ambitions they cherish should clash. There cannot be two kings in Brentford. There cannot be two Imperial powers in Europe. There is an inherent antagonism between Hitler's aims and Mussolini's.

Western Mail, Saturday, 15 March 1941

hardened thugs. Many were drawn from Heydrich's thinktank pool. Almost half were PhD graduates, with SS-Brigadeführer und Generalmajor der Polizei Dr Otto Rasch, commander of Einsatzgruppe C, a holder of two PhDs. Einsatzgruppe C commander, SS-Gruppenführer und Generalleutnant der Polizei Dr Otto Ohlendorf, a leading economist, was another example of the university-qualified and loyal intellectuals that Heydrich had at his immediate disposal from a talented officer staff. Others were experts in the field of criminal and racial law, but every officer, to the man, was well-qualified in his incorruptible passion for the Nazi cause. They were also youthful, mostly born between 1900 and 1915, and recruited as young graduates in the formative years of the Nazi movement between 1933 and 1937.

Subsequent to the selection process, inherent leadership qualities were nurtured and channelled into extracting out of their subordinates the legitimate and unhesitating physical enactment of the Führer's vision: killing Jews and other categories of 'troublemakers' such as partisans and conspirators. Thus would the shooting of unarmed civilians be justified to attain a Utopian state.

The Einsatzgruppen formation and hierarchy at the time of the invasion and occupation of Eastern Europe comprised:

Chief of Security Police and SD, or CSSD
SS-Obergruppenführer und General der Polizei Reinhard Tristan Eugen
    Heydrich (1939–42)
SS-Obergruppenführer Erich von dem Bach-Zelewski (SS Supreme Commander,
    Central Russia)
SS-Obergruppenführer und General der Polizei Ernst Kaltenbrunner (1943–45)

Einsatzgruppe A (Army Group North – Baltic States)
Commanding officers:
SS-Brigadeführer und Generalmajor der Polizei Dr Franz Walter Stahlecker
    (1941–42)
SS-Brigadeführer und Generalmajor der Polizei Heinz Jost (1942)
SS-Oberführer und Oberst der Polizei Dr Humbert Achamer-Pifrader (1942–43)
SS-Oberführer Friedrich Panzinger (1943–44)
SS-Oberführer und Oberst der Polizei Dr Wilhelm Fuchs (1944)

Einsatzkommando 1a:
SS-Obersturmbannführer Dr Martin Sandberger (1942)
SS-Obersturmbannführer Karl Tschierschky (1942)
SS-Sturmbannführer Dr. Erich Isselhorst (1942–43)
SS-Obersturmbannführer Bernhard Baatz (1943)

Einsatzkommando 1b:
SS-Sturmbannführer Dr. Hermann Hubig (1942)
SS-Sturmbannführer Dr. Manfred Pechau (1942)

Einsatzkommando 1c:
SS-Sturmbannführer Kurt Graaf (1942)

Einsatzkommando 2:
SS-Obersturmbannführer Rudolf Batz (1941)
SS-Obersturmbannführer Dr. Eduard Strauch (1941)
SS-Sturmbannführer Dr. Rudolf Lange (1941–44)
SS-Sturmbannführer Dr. Manfred Pechau (1942)
SS-Sturmbannführer Reinhard Breder (1943)
SS-Obersturmbannführer Oswald Poche (1943–44)

Einsatzkommando 3:
SS-Standartenführer Karl Jäger (1941–1943)
SS-Oberführer und Oberst der Polizei Dr Wilhelm Fuchs (1943–44)
SS-Sturmbannführer Hans-Joachim Böhme (1944)

Einsatzgruppe B (Army Group Centre – Eastern Poland)
Commanding officers:
SS-Gruppenführer und Generalmajor der Polizei Arthur Nebe (1941)
SS-Brigadeführer und Generalmajor der Polizei Erich Naumann (1941–43)
SS-Standartenführer Horst Böhme (1943)
SS-Oberführer und Oberst der Polizei Erich Ehrlinger (1943–44)
SS-Oberführer und Oberst der Polizei Heinrich Seetzen (1944)
SS-Standartenführer Horst Böhme (1944)

Einsatzkommando 8:
SS-Obersturmbannführer Dr Otto Bradfisch (1941–42)
SS-Sturmbannführer Heinz Richter (1942)
SS-Sturmbannführer Dr. Erich Isselhorst (1942)
SS-Obersturmbannführer Hans-Gerhard Schindhelm (1942–43)
SS-Sturmbannführer Alfred Rendörffer (1944)

Einsatzkommando 9:
SS-Obersturmbannführer Alfred Filbert (1941)
SS-Obersturmbannführer Oswald Schäfer (1941–42)

SS-Obersturmbannführer Wilhelm Wiebens (1942–43)
SS-Obersturmbannführer Dr Friedrich Buchardt (1943–44)
SS-Sturmbannführer Werner Kämpf (1943–44)

Einsatzgruppe C (Army Group South – Soviet Ukraine)
Commanding officers:
SS-Brigadeführer und Generalmajor der Polizei Dr Otto Rasch (1941)
SS-Gruppenführer und Generalleutnant der Polizei Max Thomas (1941–43)
SS-Standartenführer Horst Böhme (1943–1944)

Einsatzkommando 4a:
SS-Standartenführer Paul Blobel (1941–42)
SS-Obersturmbannführer Erwin Weinmann (1942)
SS-Sturmbannführer Eugen Steimle (1942–43)
SS-Sturmbannführer Friedrich Schmidt (1943)
SS-Sturmbannführer Theodor Christensen (1943)

Einsatzkommando 4b:
SS-Obersturmbannführer Günther Herrmann (1941)
SS-Obersturmbannführer Fritz Braune (1941–42)
SS-Obersturmbannführer Dr. Walter Hänsch (1942)
SS-Obersturmbannführer August Meier (1942)
SS-Sturmbannführer Friedrich Sühr (1942–43)
SS-Sturmbannführer Waldemar Krause (1943–44)

Einsatzkommando 5:
SS-Oberführer Erwin Schulz (1941)
SS-Sturmbannführer August Meier (1941–42)

Einsatzkommando 6:
SS-Standartenführer Dr. Erhard Kröger (1941)
SS-Sturmbannführer Robert Möhr (1941–42).
SS-Obersturmbannführer Ernst Biberstein (1942–1943)
SS-Sturmbannführer Friedrich Sühr (1943)

Einsatzgruppe D (Eleventh Army – Crimea)
Commanding officers:
SS-Gruppenführer und Generalleutnant der Polizei Dr Otto Ohlendorf (1941–42)
SS-Brigadeführer und Generalmajor der Polizei Walther Bierkamp (1942–43)

Einsatzkommando 10a:
SS-Oberführer und Oberst der Polizei Heinrich Seetzen (1941–42)
SS-Sturmbannführer Dr Kurt Christmann (1942–43)

Einsatzkommando 10b:
SS-Obersturmbannführer Alois Persterer (1941–42)
SS-Sturmbannführer Eduard Jedamzik (1942–43)

Einsatzkommando 11a:
SS-Obersturmbannführer Paul Zapp (1941–42)
SS-Sturmbannführer Fritz Mauer (1942)
SS-Sturmbannführer Dr Gerhard Bast (1942)
SS-Sturmbannführer Werner Hersmann (1942–43)

Einsatzkommando 11b:
SS-Sturmbannführer Hans Unglaube (1941)
SS-Obersturmbannführer Bruno Müller (1941)
SS-Obersturmbannführer Werner Braune (1941–42)
SS-Obersturmbannführer Paul Schultz (1942–43)

Einsatzkommando 12:
SS-Obersturmbannführer Gustav Adolf Nosske (1941–42)
SS-Sturmbannführer Dr. Erich Müller (1942)
SS-Obersturmbannführer Günther Herrmann (1942–43)

Einsatzgruppe E (Twelfth Army – Croatia)
Commanding officers:
SS-Obersturmbannführer Ludwig Teichmann (1941–43)
SS-Standartenführer Günther Herrmann (1943–44)
SS-Oberführer und Oberst der Polizei Wilhelm Fuchs (1944)

Einsatzkommando 10b:
SS-Obersturmbannführer und Oberregierungsrat Joachim Deumling (1943–45)
SS-Sturmbannführer Franz Sprinz (1945)

Einsatzkommando 11a:
SS-Sturmbannführer und Regierungsrat Rudolf Korndörfer (1943
SS-Obersturmbannführer Anton Fest (1943–45)

Einsatzkommando 15:
SS-Hauptsturmführer Willi Wolter (1943–44)

Einsatzkommando 16:
SS-Obersturmbannführer und Oberregierungsrat Johannes Thümmler (1943)
SS-Obersturmbannführer Joachim Freitag (1943–44)

Einsatzkommando Agram (Zagreb, Croatia):
SS-Sturmbannführer und Regierungsrat Rudolf Korndörfer (1943)

Einsatzgruppe Serbien (Serbia):
SS-Oberführer und Oberst der Polizei Wilhelm Fuchs (1941–42)
SS-Oberführer Emanuel Schäfer (1942)

Einsatzkommando Tunis (Tunisia):
Commanded by SS-Standartenführer Walter Rauff

Einsatzkommando Finnland (Finland and Norway):
Subordinate directly to Himmler and the RHSA, its wartime existence was only
   discovered in 2008.

Polish Jewess wearing the obligatory Star of David armband. (Photo Bundesarchiv)

Planned Einsatzkommando Units

Einsatzkommando 6:

To be commanded by Dr Franz Six; planned for Britain, but cancelled when re-assigned to the Soviet Union pending the capture of Moscow.

Einsatzkommando Ägypten (Egypt):

To be commanded by SS-Obersturmbannführer Walther Rauff; planned as a mobile death squad to eliminate Jews in Palestine.

NAZIS PLAN TO INVADE CRIMEA

Move to Help Drive on Kiev and Odessa
Monday
The Germans may shortly attempt an invasion of the Crimea province of South Russia with troops carried in hundreds of naval barges, according to reliable military advices from Moscow, said Martin Agronsky, the National Broadcasting Company's correspondent, broadcasting from Ankara today. The invasion would be aimed to support the big Nazi push for Kiev and Odessa. For the past few weeks the Germans have had concentrated at the Black Sea port of Constanza and at various points north of it between 250 and 300 naval barges each capable of carrying 400 shock troops complete with specialised auxiliary equipment.

"At the same time the Nazis have been concentrating at various points along the Rumanian Black Sea coast neat the Russian frontier a further 400 barges for similar troop carrying purposes," continued Agronsky.

INVASION FLEET

"Further south between 20 and 30 Rumanian and Bulgarian coastal freighters able to carry about 6,000 fully equipped shock troops are sheltering in Bulgarian ports. As a protection for this invasion fleet the Nazis have shipped by rail to Bulgarian and Rumanian points for assembly parts of some 15 to 20 extremely fast torpedo boats. In addition there are known to be at least eight German submarines already operating and ready to go into action in the Black Sea. The Nazi plan is said to be entirely dependent on the progress of the German columns, which have penetrated southeast of Kiev and are driving south towards Odessa. If the German manoeuvres succeed and Odessa is occupied, it is expected that all the German barges and ships will be moved up to Odessa and the stage will be set for the main objective of the Nazi attack in the south – the Russian Crimea and the great Soviet Crimean naval base of Sebastopol.

NAVAL LANDING

"From Odessa with aerial and E boat protection the Germans can hope to try a naval landing on the Crimea with parachute troops. They will thus side-step the powerful Soviet defence along the narrow neck of land which connects the Crimea to the Ukrainian main land and would gain a powerful operational base. The Russian High Command is fully aware of this information and it is reliably reported that large scale Russian reinforcements are being added to Marshal Budenny's Army." – Reuter.

Shields Daily News, Monday, 11 August 1941

Elderly Jews being forced to hit each other in public.

2. POWER THROUGH TERROR

'When a man's burning to death, he'll jump into any water, even though it's boiling.'

Heinrich Himmler

The Einsatzgruppen were bestowed with a wide mandate in order to accomplish their mission: 'preventive security', the eradication of those deemed to be enemies of the Reich, such as Jews, Bolsheviks and gypsies.

The Chief of the Security Police Berlin: September 21, 1939
SECRET To: Chiefs of all Einsatzgruppen of the Security Police
Subject: Jewish question in the occupied territory

I refer to the conference held in Berlin today and once more point out that the planned overall measures (i.e., the final aim) are to be kept strictly secret.

I
Distinction must be made between:
(1) The final aim (which will require extended periods of time), and
(2) The stages leading to the fulfilment of this final aim (which will be carried out in short terms).

The planned measures demand the most thorough preparation in their technical as well as economic aspects. It is obvious that the tasks that lie ahead cannot be laid down in full detail from here. The instructions and guidelines below will at the same time serve the purpose of urging the chiefs of the Einsatzgruppen to give the matter their practical thought. For the time being, the first prerequisite for the final aim is the concentration of the Jews from the countryside into the larger cities. This is to be carried out with all speed.

In doing so, distinction must be made:
(1) between the areas of Danzig and West Prussia, Posen, Eastern Upper Silesia, and
(2) the rest of the occupied territories.

As far as possible, the area mentioned (in item 1) is to be cleared of Jews; at least the aim should be to establish only a few cities of concentration.

In the areas mentioned in item 2, as few concentration points as possible are to be set up, so as to facilitate subsequent measures. In this conjunction, it is to be borne in mind that only cities which are rail junctions, or at least are located along railroad lines are to be designated as concentration points.

On principle, Jewish communities of fewer than 500 persons are to be dissolved and to be transferred to the nearest city of concentration.

This decree does not apply to the area of Einsatzgruppe 1, which is situated east of Cracow and is bounded roughly by Polanico, Jaroslaw, the new line of demarcation, and the former Slovak–Polish border. Within this area, only an improvised census of Jews is to be carried out. Furthermore, Councils of Jewish Elders, as discussed below, are to be set up.

Himmler inspects Soviet POWs. (Photo Hoffman Collection)

THE JEWS IN POLAND

Since the war started we have heard relatively little of the cruelties inflicted by the Germans on the people of Poland, but enough to know that these go on with pitiless severity. In particular, the Polish Jews, of whom there are about three millions, more than half them in the part of Poland occupied by the Germans, are suffering privations more severe even than those experienced by their fellows in Austria two years ago. The Hitler Government has declared its intention to set up a "protected Polish State" to stand as a buffer State between Germany and Russia. Into this area, still to be delineated, all the Jews in Poland are now being driven by an army of 6,000 Gestapo, and the intention is announced of adding to them during the coming year all the Jews in Germany. If the policy is realised the "protected Polish State" will be more a Jewish than a Polish State, and it will be the most poverty-stricken region in the world. The Jews now being driven towards it are compelled to leave their homes at few minutes' notice, and are allowed take nothing of their property with them.

Dundee Courier, Tuesday, 7 November 1939

II

Councils of Jewish Elders [Jüdische Ältestenräte]

(1) In each Jewish community, a Council of Jewish Elders is to be set up, to be composed, as far as possible, of the remaining influential personalities and rabbis. The council is to comprise up to 24 male Jews (depending on the size of the Jewish community). The council is to be made fully responsible, in the literal sense of the word, for the exact punctual execution of all directives issued or yet to be issued.

(2) In case of sabotage of such instructions, the councils are to be warned of the severest measures.

(3) The Jewish councils are to take an improvised census of the Jews in their local areas – broken down if possible by sex (age groups): a) up to 16 years of age, b) from 16 to 20 years of age, and c) over, as well as by principal occupation groups – and are to report the results in the shortest possible time.

(4) The Councils of Elders are to be informed of the dates and deadlines for departure, departure facilities, and finally departure routes. They are then to be made personally responsible for the departure of the Jews from the countryside.

Ordnungspolizei rounding up Jews in a *razzia* (planned raid) for registration and concentration in the Kraków ghetto. (Photo Bundesarchiv)

The reason to be given for the concentration of the Jews into the cities is that Jews have most influentially participated in guerrilla attacks and plundering actions.

(5) The Councils of Elders in the cities of concentration are to be made responsible for appropriately housing the Jews moving in from the countryside.

For general reasons of security, the concentration of Jews in the cities will probably necessitate orders altogether barring Jews from certain sections of cities, or, for example, forbidding them to leave the ghetto or go out after a designated evening hour, etc. However, economic necessities are always to be considered in this connection.

(6) The Councils of Elders are also to be made responsible for appropriate provisioning of the Jews during the transport to the cities.

No objections are to be voiced in the event that migrating Jews take their movable possessions with them, to the extent that this is technically possible.

(7) Jews who do not comply with the order to move into the cities are to be allowed a short additional period of grace where circumstances warrant. They are to be warned of strictest punishment if they should fail to comply with this latter deadline.

III

On principle, all necessary measures are always to be taken in closest accord and cooperation with the German civil administration agencies and locally competent military authorities. In carrying them out, care must be taken that the economic security of the occupied territories not be impaired.

(1) Above all, the needs of the army must be considered. For example, for the time being it will hardly be possible to avoid leaving behind some Jew traders here and there, who in the absence of other possibilities simply must

stay for the sake of supplying the troops. In such cases, however, prompt Aryanization of these enterprises is to be sought and the emigration of the Jews is to be completed later, in accord with the locally competent German administrative authorities.

(2) For the preservation of German economic interests in the occupied territories, it is obvious that Jewish-owned essential or war industries and enterprises, as well as those important for the Four Year Plan, must be kept up for the time being. In these cases also, prompt Aryanization is to be sought, and the emigration of the Jews is to be completed later.

(3) Finally, the food situation in the occupied territories must be taken into consideration. For instance, as far as possible, real estate owned by Jewish settlers is to be provisionally entrusted to the care of neighbouring German or even Polish farmers, to be worked by them together with their own, so as to assure harvesting of the crops still in the fields or renewed cultivation. With regard to this important question, contact is to be made with the agricultural expert of the Chief of the Civil Administration.

An image from the Stroop Report, prepared by General Jürgen Stroop and originally intended as a souvenir album for Himmler, chronicling the German quashing of the Warsaw ghetto uprising and the liquidation of its inhabitants. First titled *The Jewish Quarter of Warsaw is No More!*

(4) In all cases in which the interests of the Security Police on one hand and those of the German Civil Administration on the other hand cannot be reconciled, I am to be informed in the fastest way before the particular measures in question are to be carried out, and my decision is to be awaited.

IV

The chiefs of the Einsatzgruppen will report to me continuously on the following matters:

(1) Numerical survey of the Jews present in their territories (broken down as indicated above, if possible). The numbers of Jews who are being evacuated from the countryside and of those who are already in the cities are to be reported separately.

(2) Names of the cities which have been designated as concentration points.

(3) Deadlines set for the Jews to migrate to the cities.

(4) Survey of all Jewish-owned essential or war industries and enterprises, as well as those important for the Four Year Plan, within their areas.

If possible, the following should be specified:

a. Kind of enterprise (also statement on possible conversion into enterprises that are truly essential or war related, or important for the Four Year Plan);

b. Which of these enterprises need to be Aryanized most promptly (in order to forestall any kind of loss)? What kind of Aryanization is suggested? German or Poles? (This decision depends on the importance of the enterprise.);

c. How large is the number of Jews working in these enterprises (including leading positions)? Can the enterprise simply be kept up after the removal of the Jews, or will such continued operation require assignment of German or Polish workers? On what scale?

Insofar as Polish workers have to be introduced, care should be taken that they are mainly brought in from the former German provinces, so as to begin the weeding out of the Polish element there. These questions can be carried out only through involvement and participation of the German labour offices which have been set up.

V

For the attainment of the goals set, I expect total deployment of all forces of the Security Police and the Security Service. The chiefs of neighbouring Einsatzgruppen are to establish contact with each other immediately so that the territories concerned will be covered completely.

VI

The High Command of the Army, the Plenipotentiary for the Four Year Plan (Attention: Secretary of State Neumann), the Reich Ministries of the Interior (Attention: Secretary of State Stuckart), for Food and for Economy (Attention: Secretary of State Landfried), as well as the Chiefs of Civil Administration of the Occupied Territory have all received copies of this decree.

Signed Heydrich

As the cities in Latvia, Estonia, Lithuania, Belorussia and the Ukraine fell to the Wehrmacht, the Germans discovered the bodies of nationalist leaders, murdered in their places of incarceration by the retreating Soviet secret police: the People's Commissariat for Internal Affairs, or NKVD (Narodnyi Komissariat Vnutrennikh Del).

The NKVD was both hated and feared, regarded as having orchestrated the famine of the early 1920s that resulted in the death through starvation of 5 million Ukrainians. With the arrival of the Germans and the promise of independence, the Ukrainian lust for revenge was so great that Hitler's generals merely had to harness this powerful resource to comply with the Führer's desire for a Bolshevik-free Eastern Europe. There was, of course, no intention by Berlin to re-instate Ukrainian suzerainty, but, for the moment, this delusion served their objectives.

Anti-Semitism was not new to the Ukraine. For centuries, an all-pervasive Christian hatred of Jews had been nurtured through the apportionment of blame for economic greed and corruption, seen also as being complicit in Moscow's suppression of Ukrainian nationalism.

Residents of the Latvian capital, Riga, celebrate the arrival of the Wehrmacht, all-conquering heroes of liberation from Soviet tyranny. (Photo Bundesarchiv)

43

NAZI BABY DRIVE

£10,000,000 Subsidy Plan for Marriage Loans

The Nazis now plan to spend £10,000,000 to subsidise marriages and babies. Still more substantial "marriage loans" are offered to poor couples to encourage them to wed, and part the loans will be written off as each child born. "Das Schwarze Korps," publication of Heinrich Himmler's S.S. Elite Corps, saying that every German woman should bear a child, added, "Colonies which are wresting from British moneybags call for the youthful pioneer spirit." Whether children are born in or out of wedlock is not considered important, as long as they are "racially pure." "Das Schwarze Korps" praised the Mayor of Wattenscheid, in Prussia, who has begun a campaign to induce single women over 29 to bear children as "a sacrifice to the nation." Under the Nazi system the birth control movement naturally finds place. Abortion laws are strictly enforced, with imprisonment up five years for mothers and 15 years for doctors. – Associated Press.

Yorkshire Evening Post, Wednesday, 19 November 1941

Exploiting this latent anti-Jewish zeal, Berlin's secret intelligence machinery quietly fed news of an imminent German invasion into the Eastern European nationalist cells, and, in doing so, ignited an inferno of terror on the Jews across the breadth of the continent.

In June 1941, thousands of Jews were set upon and murdered in the streets of Riga, capital city of Latvia, Lithuania's capital Vilnius and second largest city Kaunas, and in the towns and cities of Ukrainian regions Lviv and Galicia.

For Heydrich and his Einsatzgruppen death squads, this upsurge of nationalism in the void left by the retreating Soviet armies provided an ideal kick-start for their programme of Jewish and Bolshevik annihilation: keen and very willing hands were not in short supply.

In Kaunas, several hundred Jews were dragged out their houses to clean up – by hand – manure left by German horses. Lithuanians, wearing white armbands to identify them as nationalists, then beat the bewildered Jews to death with clubs. German troops stood idly by, watching the savagery with a throng of Kaunas spectators that included women and children. Some played music, others

Zusammengetrieben –
'herding together' – Libau
(Liepāja), Latvia, 1941.
(Photo Bundesarchiv)

Ostland Reichskommissar
Hinrich Lohse (centre) and
fellow senior officers at the
Riga train station.
(Photo Bundesarchiv)

took photographs. In the ensuing few weeks, thousands more died in the Kaunas pogrom at the hands of Lithuanian nationalists.

This scenario would be repeated on 27 June 1941 with the arrival of Einsatzgruppen C in Lviv in the Ukraine, where the resident Jewish community stood at 160,000. The Germans widely publicized their discovery of the corpses of Ukrainian nationalists in a fortress on the outskirts of the city. The buildings and walled courtyards of Brygidki Prison, used by the Soviet NKVD, now became the blood-drenched destiny of hundreds of Jews, bludgeoned to death by fanatic Ukrainian nationalists. Many of the male orthodox Jews had their beards and *peyot* (sidelocks) set alight before being murdered.

Rounding up male Polish Jews. (Photo Bundesarchiv)

Nazi anti-Semitic propaganda was ramped up to against the Eastern European Jews, accusing them of being 'homicidal scum' who had worked in collaboration with the NKVD. 'Liberated' citizens of the German-occupied territories were exhorted to hand over these traitors to the nationalist cause to German troops for 'punishment'. They were labelled Jewish Soviet 'looters and marauders ... allies of Churchill and his plutocratic clique'. Propaganda films showed naked women running a gauntlet of club-wielding Ukrainians, while others were pulled through the streets by their hair. The occupying forces had granted the Ukrainians full licence to exert their power over the Jews through terror and mass murder.

At Tarnopol (Ternopil from 1944), east of Lviv, elements of the 5th Waffen-SS Wiking Panzer Division teamed up with forces of Ukrainian nationalists under Stepan 'Hero of Ukraine' Bandera to conduct similar acts of terror and slaughter of Jews. For the first time, members of the SS Totenkopf, or Death's Head, assumed a leading role in the massacres.

There was, however, a concurrently growing concern among heads of the Einsatzgruppen that this random and undisciplined addressing of the Jewish question by aggrieved, bloodthirsty nationalists was not the answer – it lacked German efficiency. Reports from Einsatzgruppen at the time highlighted such shortcomings: 'To this day in Kaunas, 7,800 Jews have been liquidated, partially through pogroms and partially through shootings organized by Lithuanian commandos. The inhabitants of Lemberg [German name for Lviv] eliminated approximately 1,000 Jews in the GPU [NKVD] prison that is currently occupied by the Wehrmacht.'

The Einsatzgruppen now saw the need to standardize and streamline the whole eradication process.

3. DEATH WAS THEIR TOOL

Black milk of daybreak we drink you at night
we drink you at noon death is a master from Germany
we drink you at nightfall and morning we drink and drink
death is a master from Germany with eyes that are blue
with a bullet of lead he will hit in the mark he will hit you
a man in the house your golden hair Margarete
he hunts us down with his dogs in the sky he gives us a grave
he plays with the serpents and dreams death is a master from Germany.

Paul Celan's Todesfuge (Death Fugue)

For some time, Hitler had considered the mass exportation of the 4 million Jews in German-occupied territories to an overseas country. The island of Madagascar, mooted at the end of the nineteenth century by several European countries in which to establish a Jewish colony, was one such option.

In Berlin on 3 July 1940, head of the Jewish Affairs desk in the foreign ministry, Franz Rademacher, submitted his proposals for the Madagascar Plan:

The approaching victory gives Germany the possibility, and in my view also the duty, of solving the Jewish question in Europe. The desirable solution is: all Jews out of Europe.

Section D III proposes as a solution of the Jewish question: In the Peace Treaty France must make the island of Madagascar available for the solution of the Jewish question, and to resettle and compensate the approximately 25,000 French citizens living there. The island will be transferred to Germany under a mandate. Diégo Suarez Bay and the port of Antsirane, which are strategically important, will become German naval bases (if the Navy wishes, these naval bases could be extended also to the harbours – open road-steads – Tamatave, Andevorante, Mananjara, etc.).

In addition to these naval bases, suitable areas of the country will be excluded from the Jewish territory (Judenterritorium) for the construction of air bases. That part of the island not required for military purposes will be placed under the administration of a German Police Governor, who will be under the administration of the Reichsführer SS. Apart from this, the Jews will have their own administration in this territory: their own mayors, police, postal and railroad administration, etc. The Jews will be jointly liable for the value of the island. For this purpose, their former European financial assets will be transferred for use to a European bank to be established for this purpose. Insofar as the assets are not sufficient to pay for the land which they will receive, and for the purchase of necessary commodities in Europe for the development of the island, the Jews will be able to receive bank credits from the same bank.

As Madagascar will only be a Mandate, the Jews living there will not acquire German citizenship. On the other hand, the Jews deported to Madagascar will lose their citizenship of European countries from the date of deportation. Instead, they will become residents of the Mandate of Madagascar.

This arrangement would prevent the possible establishment in Palestine by the Jews of a Vatican State of their own, and the opportunity for them to exploit for their own purposes the symbolic importance which Jerusalem has for the Christian and Mohammedan parts of the world. Moreover, the Jews will remain in German hands as a pledge for the future good behaviour of the members of their race in America.

Use can be made for propaganda purposes of the generosity shown by Germany in permitting cultural, economic, administrative and legal self-administration to the Jews; it can be emphasized at the same time that our German sense of responsibility towards the world forbids us to make the gift of a sovereign state to a race which has had no independent state for thousands of years: this would still require the test of history.

Processing of Jewish citizens of Warsaw.

EYES ON MADAGASCAR

Now that French West Africa has decided to fight on, Madagascar is expected soon to follow the good example of these territories. That spacious island which has been a French colony for fifty years, is far beyond the reach of the men Vichy. It could be self-contained and self-supporting if necessity dictated, but in fact does a considerable export trade in hides and rare metals – which in peace time more than paid for its imports. More to the point at the moment is the fact that, in addition to the French Civil Service and business men in its ports and capital, there is a considerable French army that has had no direct contact with the European war, and has not been disbanded. Madagascar was not, so far as is known, mentioned in the armistice terms of Germany and Italy. Even if it were, neither Hitler nor Mussolini has the sea power to reach into the South Indian Ocean.

Birmingham Daily Post, Saturday, 31 August 1940

Many believe that this was simply a ploy by Hitler to dupe the international community into believing that the munificent leader of the German people wished to grant European Jews self-determination in their own land.

By the time of the specially convened Wannsee Conference on 10 February 1942 to decide on the 'Final Solution', Rademacher's estimates of European Jews had significantly increased to almost 7 million. The shipping logistics became imponderable and it would take more than four years to translocate Europe's Jews to Madagascar. Heydrich therefore shelved the plan, replacing it with an 'evacuation to the east'.

In the interim, toward the end of July 1941 SS-Obergruppenführer Reinhard Heydrich had received a memorandum from Reichsmarschall Hermann Göring. Head of the Reichssicherheitshauptamt (Reich Main Security Office, or RSHA) Heydrich was ordered to commence making plans for the implementation of the 'Final Solution' to the Jewish question. This would, in the first instance, require the segregation of all Jews from society, followed by the obligatory registration and marking of every individual. Cut off from urban communities, fenced-off ghettos would be created into which all Jews would be translocated. Not only would this then provide a pool of slave labour, but the slums would also significantly enhance the expediency of the whole process of annihilation.

A group of the almost 2,800 mainly Serb men and boys massacred in Kragujevac being led to their execution, October 1941.

The Einsatzgruppen moved in and multiple gallows sprang up overnight. Jews, Communists and partisans were hanged in the public squares of towns and cities that history would remember as places of mass murder: Kharkov, Odessa, Kiev, Minsk. The lifeless bodies were left hanging for hours, with public notices around their necks proclaiming '*Diese Juden haben gegen die Deutsche Wehrmacht gehetzt*' – 'These Jews agitated against the German military'.

In Lviv, western Ukraine, where the majority of the population was Jewish, the Einsatzgruppe resorted to depraved theatrical spectacles in a macabre mockery of their victims as they walked to their deaths. Passion play-themed and festival-style processions provided the city's burghers with crude entertainment as the column of Jews was guided to Janovski cemetery. A German officer would select a Jew at random and 'crown' him Tsar. The bewildered man would be tarred and feathered and placed in an armchair that was his throne. Four men were then forced to carry their 'king' on their shoulders and placed at the head of the column. Those following were obliged to pay homage in song.

At a preselected, secluded area of level ground behind the cemetery, a trench had been dug and bridged with two logs. The Jews were ordered to walk on to the logs while a machine gun was being readied – they offered no resistance, they did not protest. The rude, rhythmic clattering of the machine gun shattered the false calm, sending crying and wailing men, women and children crumbling into heaps in the trench. Those who had only sustained flesh wounds to their arms and legs tried to scramble up the walls of the trench to escape the carnage. They did not succeed.

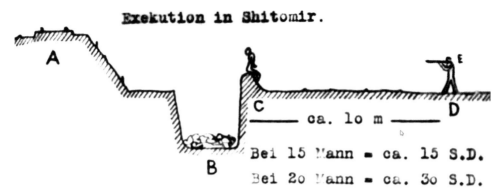

Exekution in Shitomir.

ca. 1o m

Bei 15 Mann = ca. 15 S.D.
Bei 2o Mann = ca. 3o S.D.

A German sketch detailing the methodology to be employed in trench murders.

This method of trench mass-execution increased the speed at which the Einsatzgruppen commanders were able to fulfil their quotas of Jews killed, and was increasingly employed throughout Eastern Europe.

At this point in time, Generalfeldmarschall Gerd von Rundstedt, commander of German Army Group South, distanced the Wehrmacht from the Final Solution activities of Heydrich's death squads. For von Rundstedt, a career army officer of the old Prussian school, it could never be the work of a soldier to kill in non-combatant situations.

High Command
Army Group South
Ic/AO (Abw. III)
H.Q., September 24, 1941

Re: The Struggle against Elements Hostile to the Reich
The investigation of and struggle against tendencies and elements hostile to the Reich (Communists, Jews, etc.), insofar as they are not a part of a hostile military force is, in the occupied areas, exclusively the task of the Sonderkommando (Special Unit) of the Security Police and the SD, which will take the necessary measures on their own responsibility and carry them out.

Individual actions by members of the Wehrmacht or participation by members of the Wehrmacht in excesses by the Ukrainian population against the Jews is forbidden; they are also forbidden to watch or take photographs of measures taken by the Sonderkommando.

This prohibition is to be made known to the members of all units. [Commanders] in charge of discipline at all levels are responsible for the implementation of this prohibition. In the event of breaches, it is to be investigated in every case whether the commander failed to carry out his duty of supervision, and when necessary he is to be severely punished.

Signed von Rundstedt

A career Nazi who had been appointed head of SS Group South when the NASDP came to power in 1933, in 1941 SS-Obergruppenführer Friedrich Jeckeln was transferred from Regiment 2 of the Totenkopf Division to the position of Higher SS and Police Leader of German Ostland. The ruthless Nazi immediately set about developing the eponymous 'Jeckeln System' for the systematic and efficient process of Jewish annihilation, each step in the procedure overseen and performed by specialists. Most knew it as *sardinenpackung*, or 'sardine packing'.

Members of the SD would initiate the *aktion* by rounding up the intended victims from a cordoned-off ghetto, organizing them in columns of 500 to 1,000. They would then be herded onto trucks and taken to the killing grounds where Ordnungspolizei (Order Police, or Orpo) took over.

The Orpo would then escort smaller columns to where three pits had already been dug for the next step in the process. After being instructed to discard all their clothing, footwear and valuables, the naked men, women and children had to run a gauntlet of guards to the killing pits where they were forced to lie face down, more often than not, on top of just-slaughtered bodies.

While some killers stood on the lip of the pits to fire down into their victims, others preferred to perform their grisly acts by clambering in among the living and the dead and shooting them in the back of the head at close range. Depending

Transportation to mass-murder sites.

on the Einsatzgruppe responsible, checks were not always conducted if any of those shot were still alive before filling in the pit with soil.

With the shelving of the Madagascar Plan, for Adolf Hitler only one option remained: the total and indiscriminate annihilation of Jews and Bolsheviks from all corners of the Reich. In the newly acquired Eastern European territories – key to his grand design for Aryan *Lebensraum* – Jews were stripped of even the most basic human rights and ostracized from the community at large. Since 1918, overwhelmingly convinced that Jews had masterminded the German defeat in the Great War, humiliation and a burgeoning want for revenge had haunted his every waking moment. Addressing the German parliament, the Reichstag, in 1939, Hitler was unequivocal in publicly declaring his mission: 'Today, I shall make a prophecy: if international and Jewish financiers inside and outside Europe succeed in plunging the nations into a new world war, the result will not be world Bolshevization, and thus the victory of Jewry. The result will be extermination of the Jewish race in Europe!'

However, only Jewish males deemed of an age to bear arms against the Reich would be targeted. It would only be from July 1941 with the Wehrmacht's Eastern European campaign that women and children would be included in his imperative of a 'free' Europe.

Heinrich Himmler followed right behind the German forces that were powering their way into the Soviet republics. He wished to personally discuss pogrom strategies with his Einsatzgruppen commanders. From the Baltic States to the Ukraine, the Einsatzkommando death squads were ordered to simultaneously commence operations. The targets would not have the benefit of prior warning to evade containment and death.

It was during this foundation tour that Himmler exhorted his Einsatzgruppen commanders to 'drive the women into the swamps,' a euphemism for the inclusion of Jewish women in the pogrom. Whilst the irony was not lost on members of his inner circle, Himmler was understood by most to be referring to the Jewish populations of the nine raions – administrative departments – of the Belorussian and the three of the Ukrainian Soviet republics in the region of the Pripyat River and swamps.

Operation Pripiatsee became the first systematically planned and implemented mass-murder operation of the war. Höherer SS-und Polizeiführer (Higher SS and Police Leader, or HSSPF) Erich von dem Bach-Zelewski was entrusted with the conduct of the operation on Himmler's behalf. From the end of July and well into August 1941, the SS Cavalry Brigade, and the 162nd and 252nd infantry divisions performed a two-stage extermination of more than 17,000 people.

Early in August 1941, Order No. 42 arrived from Himmler's desk: exterminate all male Jews over the age of 14, and drive the women and children into

WHAT "LEBENSRAUM" MEANS

[Secretary of State for War] Mr. Stanley, who, when he rose, was loudly cheered, said that we had, for some years, seen arising a new philosophy, a new ethic in international affairs which, if they continued, and if they were allowed to dominate us, would mean the end of the world as we knew it. For centuries we had seen a Europe which was not equally divided between a few great Powers, but which was made up countries of varying size and varying strength. Each country, small as well as large, had developed its own language, its own customs, its own ideals, its own national life, and on the whole the rights of each had been respected. Only too often wrongs, real or imaginary, had caused an appeal to arms; peaces just and unjust had been made, but only at rare intervals, and never for a hundred years had small countries lost the right to live and become the natural prey of their stronger neighbours. Yet that was the doctrine which the Nazis preached when they were weak and practised when they were strong.

Mr. Stanley continued: "You have heard a great deal about the doctrine, under the high-sounding name of Lebensraum – living room. Put more simply that doctrine only means that anything your neighbour owns is yours when you are strong enough to take it. Instance after instance has shocked the world, until the tragic history culminated in the march on Prague."

Yorkshire Post and Leeds Intelligencer, Monday, 5 February 1940

Stripped and humiliated before being shot.

the swamps to drown. The latter 'solution' proved problematic as the swamps were too shallow, so the intended victims were shot instead. This was one of the first instances of the mass murder of entire Jewish communities in what would become known as the Holocaust, or Shoah.

In the wake of the Reichsführer's whistle-stop crusade in Belorussia, there was a tangible rise in the momentum of the *aktion*, particularly the extermination of Jews in Riga and Minsk by Einsatzgruppe B, commanded by SS-Gruppenführer und Generalmajor der Polizei Arthur Nebe, aided by the SS Cavalry Brigade to augment the small forty- to fifty-strong Einsatzkommandos.

Regardless of the method of mass slaughter, consolidation and containment was the common prerequisite to ensure optimum efficacy of the eradication process. The infamous ghettos, synonymous with the Holocaust, became the staging posts. Travelling through the Jewish ghetto in Łódź, Poland, early in November 1939, Reich propaganda minister Joseph Goebbels wrote in his diary: 'We get out and inspect everything in detail. It is indescribable. These are not human beings anymore, they are animals. This therefore is no longer a humanitarian undertaking, but a surgical one. We must make radical incisions here, otherwise all of Europe will succumb to this Jewish disease. It already looks like Asia. We will have to do much to make this territory German.'

A week after the German invasion of Poland that triggered the Second World War, the city of Łódź capitulated after a frantic but futile attempt by its citizens at defending their city. With a Jewish population of 230,000, Łódź was home to one of the largest concentrations of Jews in Europe, second only to Warsaw.

On 2 November, with the incorporation of the city into the Reich, its name was changed to Litzmannstadt, and on the 16th, all Jews in the city were compelled to wear an armband on their right arm, a race identification label that would, a month later, be replaced with the yellow Star of David cloth patch.

By early December, the Nazi governor of the Kalisz- Łódź District, Friedrich Übelhör, had put his thoughts on paper for the utilization of ghettos in which to concentrate Jews prior to the implementation of the process of eradication. Ghettos already existed in parts of Poland, but there was no restriction of movement in or out of these generally depraved areas.

Initially, and working in conjunction with Łódź's law enforcement bodies, Übelhör set aside a 4.3-square-kilometre zone in the north of the city for the establishment of a ghetto.

Following a proclamation the previous month to the effect that the ghetto was riddled with infectious diseases so as to keep non-Jews out, on 8 February 1940 the instrument for the establishment of the Łódź ghetto was promulgated. Populating the ghetto by force began immediately, allowing the Jewish citizens only minutes to pack what they could for the translocation. The new

The sealed Riga ghetto.
(Photo Bundesarchiv)

NAZI TROUBLES IN POLAND

"Traitor" Germans Stand by Workers
The existence of labour troubles in Polish territory incorporated in Germany has been disclosed in a speech made to a gathering of Nazi party instructors in Lodz by the "Hauptbefehlsleiter" Schmidt, says the Polish Telegraph Agency. Schmidt referred to traitors in the German working classes, particularly among the German workers of Catholic faith, who have shown their solidarity with the Polish workers on the questions of working hours and wages. A significant example of the discrimination made between Poles and Germans by the German authorities in incorporated territories is the Children's Milk Regulation, issued by the Chief of Police in Lodz.

ANTI-JEWISH MEASURES

German children up to the age of 15 are allowed half pint of milk a day. Polish children, however, are allowed the same amount until the age of five only. Moreover, the regulation forbids Poles to buy any milk until after 9 a.m., when practically all the milk has been already bought up. The German authorities in Warsaw have forbidden Jews to leave the ghetto without a special pass authorizing them to visit other parts of the city. All credit and savings institutions have been liquidated by the German authorities in Poland and all their assets confiscated by the German Treasury. – P.A. Special.

Western Morning News, Friday, 29 November 1940

residents were crammed into the delineated confines of the ghetto, averaging 3.5 persons per room.

In April, the ghetto was fenced off, and on 1 May 1940, the war only eight months old, Übelhör sealed the ghetto and appointed a *Judenälteste* – elder of the Jews – to run the Nazi-controlled affairs of the ghetto.

On 6 January 1942, the systematic 'deportation' process commenced. Dubbed 'wedding invitations', ghetto residents were selected in batches of 1,000 for transport to the Chelmno (also known as Kulmhof) death camp, fifty miles away. Here, SS-Sturmbannführer Herbert Lange and a unit of SS-Sonderkommando perpetrated the first mass killings of Jews by carbon monoxide poisoning in what were known as 'gas vans', or *einsatzwagen*.

Lange first arrived in Poland in September 1939 with Einsatzgruppe VI (Wielkopolska) which, at the time, was commanded by SS-Oberführer Erich Naumann. Placed in command of the eponymous SS-Sonderkommando Lange early in 1940, Lange gained killing experience during his eradication of mentally ill patients and Polish civilians in Wielkopolska, Owińska, Kościan and Działdowo. Victims were generally shot in the back of the neck.

As chief of the Gestapo in German-occupied Poznań, Lange would become responsible for the murders of hundreds of Poles in the formative days of the death camp, Fort VII, officially titled Konzentrationslager Posen. Established in one of the nineteenth-century forts around the city, it was here that the mobile gas-chamber mechanism, the gas van, was first introduced, a concept that originated from an idea by Einsatzgruppe B Commander, SS-Brigadeführer (future SS-Gruppenführer und Generalmajor der Polizei) Arthur Nebe.

A Magirus-Deutz furniture van converted into killing by poisonous exhaust fumes.

Tasked with liquidating greater numbers of patients in asylums in the Belorussian cities of Minsk and Mogilev, Nebe sought an alternative to shooting. He considered two options: explosives and gas. Dr Albert Widmann, a chemist at the Technical Institute for the Detection of Crime (Kriminaltechnisches Institut der Sicherheitspolizei, or KTI), duly arrived at Minsk equipped with 400kg of explosives and metal piping to find which was the most effective method of mass killing.

In a forest on the outskirts of Minsk, twenty-five mental patients were locked into a bunker containing explosives. However, the first detonation only killed a few, requiring a second explosion to finish the test with 100 per cent fatalities. Clearly, the use of explosives was not an option.

A few days thereafter, Nebe and Widmann went to the asylum at Mogilev to conduct tests on the efficacy of poison gas. A room at the hospital was hermetically sealed and around thirty patients placed inside. A pipe in the wall connected to a running car's exhaust, introduced carbon monoxide into the room, but after eight minutes, the intended victims had not succumbed to the toxic gas. A second

Jewish women and children 'deported' to Auschwitz. (Photo Bundesarchiv)

ATROCITIES IN POLAND

From a Special Correspondent

The atrocities of the German barbarians in Poland have surpassed even those of Attila, the Hun.

Accounts of unnameable horrors – all authenticated by names, places, and dates – reached me yesterday by a route which cannot be disclosed. Many of these horrors are too bestial for print. The Hun is slowly but surely converting Polish girls into prostitution. He takes a sadistic pleasure in kidnapping delicately nurtured girls. At least seventy were seized in the streets of Cracow, Suchedniow and Siedlce in September and sent to "houses." Those who resisted were beaten until they died. In April last year scores of girls, little more than children, living in Syrokomla and Ozdsieszow, were foully assaulted by a gang of soldiers in the presence of their mothers and then shot.

The fifteen-year-old daughter a Warsaw judge was bestially tortured for twelve days. In August two Warsaw girls, aged fourteen and sixteen, were found with Polish leaflets in their possession. They were put in prison and at the end of three weeks were returned dead to their parents. Their bodies bore marks of torture. Two boys, aged nine and eleven, were shot on September 24 at Suwalki. They were suspected of knowing where arms were hidden and refused to disclose information.

Four hundred inmates of an asylum in Chelm Lubin province were machine-gunned because the Gestapo wanted the building for themselves. Last winter the old people, cripples, and weak-minded children of Rosana and Makow and of the adjoining villages were taken to a wood and shot. This was also the fate of forty-two old men, inmates of a home at Plock. Scores of old, ill, and insane people have been poisoned in a gas chamber in a fort in Poznan.

There are also numerous known instances of the sterilisation of boys and girls, and 1,000 youths and girls of good families were deported from Teschen, Silesia, after being imprisoned and beaten for four days. They had only one meal a day and for nine hours on end were forced to stand facing a wall with armed sentries guarding them. In Bytom two Poles suspected of being officers in disguise were hanged together in a main street in such a way that when one's feet touched the ground the other was lifted into the air. This ghastly "see-saw" went on for an hour until the men died. A large crowd demonstrated against this act of gross brutality, but it went on just the same.

Aberdeen Press and Journal, Tuesday, 29 April 1941

car was connected to another pipe embedded in the wall and, working in tandem with the first vehicle, the Einsatzgruppe commander and the chemist achieved the desired result.

Following the success of the latter experiment, Nebe conceived the idea of a mobile gassing vehicle, where victims would be loaded into a sealed cab on a vehicle into which the exhaust fumes from the engine would be piped. The 'euthanasia' process, taking up to thirty minutes, would take place during the journey from loading point to burial site. Heydrich endorsed the concept.

Two models of gas van, resembling ambulances or refrigerated trucks, were produced by car manufacturer, Gabschat Farengewerke GmbH in Berlin – one with a densely packed capacity of up to 100 people, the other up to 150. Toward the end of 1941, the gas vans were supplied to the Einsatzgruppen and the Chelmno death camps. The success of gassing experimentation would also manifest itself in the construction of permanent gas chambers in extermination camps such as Auschwitz, Dachau, Sachsenhausen and Majdanek.

Arrest and public humiliation of Polish Jews during an SS raid near Lublin, c. 1940. (Source Gestapo Museum, Berlin)

4. MASS SLAUGHTER

The day after Germany launched its attack on the Soviet Union on 22 June 1941, the Security Service (SD) of the RSHA immediately went into action, arresting 114 Poles and White Russians. A further 906 Soviet nationals were detained on the 24th, and by 3 July 1941, in their drive to neutralize NKVD activities, 4,995 Soviet citizens were reported to be under arrest.

As the German military advanced, so did teams of the SD and Einsatzgruppen. However, very few NKVD documents were captured, the Germans discovering, upon reaching NKVD installations, that files had been removed or destroyed. However, based on prior intelligence, they did manage to execute a large number of arrests.

Moscow, however, with its traditional lines of intelligence flow from the west severely disrupted by the invading German armies and the aggressive activities of the SD, desperately needed to fill the void and reconstitute essential intelligence on the movements of Hitler's forces. On 3 August 1941, 250 members of the 212th Soviet Parachute Brigade were dropped behind the German lines in Belorussia and West Ukraine. A week later, another 200 agents were deployed by air behind German lines between Równo and Łuck, but most of them were quickly rounded up by the SD. Undeterred, the Soviets continued to pour hundreds of agents into German-occupied territories. The SD added these agents to the growing lists of those 'elements hostile' to Nazi domination who required neutralizing or exterminating, but the liquidation of Jews in the 'final solution' remained the top priority.

'Bloody Sunday', in which the killing of Germans by Poles took place in Bydgoszcz, a Polish city with a sizable German minority, in September 1939. A windfall for Nazi propaganda, retaliation was swift and brutal. (Photo Bundesarchiv)

With the deployment of Einsatzgruppen from the Baltic to the Black Sea, the territorial command and reporting structure of the Nazi instruments of security and law enforcement, was split into three segments: headquarters for the northern area in Riga, Latvia, for the middle area in Mogilev, Belorussia, and for the southern area in Kiev, Ukraine. While reporting directly to the RHSA headquarters in Berlin, these three commands were designated Einsatzgruppen and Einsatzkommandos.

By January 1942, the SD estimated that some 500 Soviet agents still remained at large in the occupied Leningrad area alone. Berlin had good reason to expect more – in Mogilev they had captured photographs of about 1,000 agents who had been trained at an NKVD school in that area. From 31 July 1941 to 2 April 1943, the arrest of 3,742 Soviet agents was recorded, in addition to 365 individuals listed as communists. A far larger number of communists were liquidated in the mass executions that occurred under the auspices of the Nazi programme for political and ethnic purification of the occupied territories.

With the launch of Operation Barbarossa, mass executions commenced almost immediately on the Eastern Front. A great majority of the persons thus liquidated were Jews, but occasional executions of communists, NKVD agents and Soviet partisans were included. Generally, the units in the field merely listed their victims as 'Jews' or 'mostly Jews' – no evidence has been found that would suggest that Berlin demanded more precise reporting. The SD teams led the actions as well doing the reporting, even though a police battalion may have performed the actual executing, such as the one which slaughtered 2,000 Jews and Russians in the Czebetowska area in early August 1941.

Executions of Jews by Einsatzgruppen near Ivangorod, Ukraine, 1942.

Einsatzgruppe A, situated farther north, reported the execution of 29,000 persons in the rear areas of Latvia and Lithuania at about the same time. SS Sturmbannführer H. Barth had been commended for directing the action 'in an outstanding manner' when he organized the execution of 2,300 Jews in Riga in July 1941.

Daily, the *Aktion* programme of mass extermination continued without relent – in Grodno, in Słonin, in Kishinev. In July and August 1941 alone, a total of 150,000 executions were listed in the reports to Berlin. On a September report covering Einsatzgruppe C, someone had annotated, '50,000 executions foreseen in Kiev'.

RSHA headquarters, in turn, consolidated such statistical data from field operations, which was disseminated in periodic study reviews to forty-eight different Nazi addresses. Within the reviews, the RSHA would make occasional references to the attitude of local populations in occupied territories towards the anti-Jewish programme. Only the Latvians were reported to be 'not very enthusiastic' about the campaigns, while the dubbed 'self-defence forces' of Latvia, as well as those of Lithuania and Estonia, were extensively used to carry out executions. The West Ukrainians were also overt supporters of anti-Jewish action and, as such, readily volunteered to assist. In Dobrómyl they set fire to a Jewish synagogue, while in Sambor they mobbed some fifty Jews.

In the town of Lwów (Lviv in Ukrainian and Lemberg in German) in German-occupied Poland, there was no shortage of Ukrainians wishing to vent their anger and revenge against up to 300,000 Polish Jews who had initially escaped the German occupation of western Poland. In terms of the bogus German–Soviet non-aggression pact of 23 August 1939, after Hitler's armies triggered the Second World War by invading Poland from the west and after the massive influx of Jewish refugees, the Soviet Union annexed the Polish territory of Kresy, including the voivodeship of Lwów. For the hapless residents – Jew and non-Jew – the horrors of Soviet governance began. Supplies of corn, wheat flour, meat, sugar, salt, tobacco and matches into the city were cut overnight. During 1940, hundreds of thousands of Lwów residents, including tens of thousands of Jews, were forcibly removed to Siberia and certain oblivion.

On 30 June 1941, the German 1st Mountain Division of the 49th Army Corps routed the Soviet presence in Lwów. When opening the city's Brygidki, Łąckiego Street and Zamarstynowska Street prisons, the German troops were assailed by the rancid stench of putrefying human flesh. In the prison cellars, the decomposing work of the Soviet NKVD was stacked from floor to roof. The machinery of Reich propaganda minister Joseph Goebbels exploited the Russian carnage to the full, blaming Jews for the atrocities and encouraging local Ukrainians to exact revenge on the perpetrators.

The Chief of the Security Police and the SD Berlin
July 2, 1941
Operational Situation Report USSR No. 10
Einsatzgruppe B (1)

The 17th Army Command has suggested the use first of all of the anti-Jewish and anti-Communist Poles living in the newly-occupied areas for self-cleansing activities.

On July 1, 1941 Chief of Security Police and SD issued the following order to all Einsatzgruppen:

Order No. 2:
Poles residing in the newly-occupied Polish territories may be expected, on the basis of their experiences, to be anti-Communist and also anti-Jewish.

It is obvious that the cleansing activities have to extend first of all to the Bolsheviks and the Jews. As for the Polish intelligentsia and others, decisions can be taken later, unless there is a special reason for taking action in individual cases considered to be dangerous.

It is therefore obvious that such Poles need not be included in the cleansing action, especially as they are of great importance as elements to initiate pogroms and for obtaining information. (This depends, of course, on local conditions.)

This policy is to be applied, of course, to all similar cases. Einsatzgruppe staff have arrived on July 1, at 5 am, in Lvov. Office is in the NKVD central building.

Chief of Einsatzgruppe B reports that Ukrainian insurrection movements were bloodily suppressed by the NKVD on June 25, 1941 in Lvov. About 3,000 were shot by NKVD. Prison burning. Hardly 20% of Ukrainian intelligentsia has remained. Some elements of the Bandera-group (2) under the direction of Stechko and Ravlik have organized a militia force and a municipal office. The Einsatzgruppe has created a counterbalance to the Bandera group, a Ukrainian self-policed city administration. Further measures against the Bandera-group, in particular against Bandera himself, are in preparation. They will be carried out as soon as possible.

EK 4a and EK 4b with Einsatzgruppe staff have also arrived in Lvov.

Erschiessungskommando: execution of partisans by firing squad in northern Russia. (Photo Bundesarchiv)

Goebbels's seeds of anti-Semitic hatred fell on extremely fertile soil that was the zealousness of Ukrainian nationalism. The arrival of the Wehrmacht and Einsatzgruppen C was feted in a festivity of cheering, adulation, banners and flowers – the Swastika was hoisted side by side with the Ukrainian Tryzub. In July 1941, some 6,000 Ukrainian Jewish males were murdered by Ukrainian nationals in a 'holocaust-by-bullets' pogrom directed by SS death squads.

An eye-witness account of one of these actions has been given by a German engineer based in the Ukraine:

Shortly after 2200 hours the ghetto was encircled by a large SS detachment and about three times as many members of the Ukrainian militia. Then the electric arc lights which had been erected in and around the ghetto were switched on.

SS and militia squads of 4 to 6 men entered or at least tried to enter the houses. Where the doors and windows were closed and the inhabitants did not open at the knocking, the SS men and the militia broke the windows, forced the doors with beams and crowbars, and entered the houses. The people living there were driven on to the street just as they were, regardless of whether they were dressed or in bed. Since the Jews in most cases refused to leave their houses and resisted, the SS and militia applied force. With strokes of the whip, kicks, and blows with rifle butts, they finally succeeded in clearing the houses. The people were driven out of their houses in such haste that in several instances small children in bed had been left behind.

In the street women cried out for their children and children for their parents. That did not prevent the SS from driving the people along the road at running pace, and hitting them, until they reached a waiting freight train. Car after car was filled, and the screams of the women and children and the cracking of whips and rifle shots re-sounded unceasingly. Since several families or groups had barricaded themselves in specially strong buildings, and the doors could not be forced with crowbars and beams, these houses were now blown open with hand grenades. Since the ghetto was near the railroad tracks in Rovno, the younger people tried to get across the tracks and over a small river in order to leave the ghetto area. As this stretch of country was beyond the range of the electric lights, it was illuminated by signal rockets. All through the night these beaten, hounded, and wounded people moved along the lighted streets. Women carried their dead children in their arms, children pulled and dragged their dead parents by their arms and legs down the road toward the train. Again and again the cries, 'Open the door! Open the door!' echoed through the ghetto.

This was merely a prelude to ghetto containment and deportation to extermination camps such as Belzec. In November, SS-Gruppenführer Fritz Katzmann established Jüdischer Wohnbezirk, into which 80,000 Jews were ordered to move. Prior to the commencement of deportation the following year, 5,000 sick and elderly Jews were taken from the ghetto and shot under the rail bridge on Pełtewna Street, dubbed the 'bridge of death' by the Jews. By the end of the war, Lwów's pre-war Jewish population of 150,000 had been redeuced to fewer than 1,000.

As touched on earlier, the Germans conducted Operation Pripiatsee in July and August 1941, with the explicit objective the annihilation of the entire Jewish

Death by machine-gun fire, generally regarded as wasteful in terms of ammunition.

The Chief of the Security Police and the SD Berlin
July 13, 1941
Operational Situation Report USSR No. 21
Einsatzgruppe B
Location: Minsk

A civilian prison camp was built in Minsk by the first troops passing through. Almost all the male inhabitants of the town were placed into it. The Einsatzgruppe was asked to screen the camp together with the Secret Field Police. The only persons who were set free were those able to clear themselves beyond reproach and who were neither politically nor criminally implicated. The remainder, left behind in the camp, will be subjected to careful investigation. 1,050 Jews were subsequently liquidated.

A Jewish committee was also formed, a ghetto was set up, and the identification of Jews on outer garments started. The Bolsheviks set free the inmates of the Minsk prison except the political ones. These were shot by the Bolsheviks before their retreat. A search has been started for the criminal prisoners who had been set free.

In Vilnius, by July 8th, the local Einsatzkommando liquidated 321 Jews. The Lithuanian Ordnungsdienst which was placed under the Einsatzkommando after the Lithuanian political police had been dissolved was instructed to take part in the liquidation of the Jews. 150 Lithuanian officials were assigned to this task. They arrested the Jews and put them into concentration camps where they were subjected the same day to Special Treatment. This work has now begun, and thus about 500 Jews, saboteurs amongst them, are liquidated daily. About 460,000 roubles in cash, as well as many valuables belonging to Jews who were subject to Special Treatment, were confiscated as property belonging to enemies of the Reich.

Einsatzkommando 2 in Vilnius has confiscated vast documentary materials in the local Jewish museum which was a branch of the central Moscow Institute for Jewish Culture.

Apart from 215 Jewish and Bolshevik officials, 15 more NKVD agents were shot in Bialystok. The NKVD office had been completely burnt down. Only in the cellar vaults was it possible to secure various lists. The executions continued all the time at the same rate. The Polish section of the population has shown it supports the executions by the Security Police by informing on Jewish, Russian, and also Polish Bolsheviks.

Only 96 Jews were executed in Grodno and Lida during the first days. I gave orders to intensify these activities. The activity of all the Kommandos has progressed satisfactorily. The liquidations, in particular, are in full swing and usually take place daily. The carrying out of the necessary liquidations is assured in every instance under any circumstances.

It emerges more and more clearly that the main responsibility lies with the rear section of the army area for the seizure of resistance groups, partisans, Red functionaries, and Jews. This is due to the gradual surfacing of fugitives who had escaped into the forests and swamps. It is, therefore, not practical to pull the Einsatzkommandos out of the area of the security sectors.

population from the territories of nine raions (departments) of Belorussia and three raions of the Ukraine in the region of the Pripyat (Pripet) River and swamps.

Acting on direct orders from Himmler, the SS Cavalry Brigade and two infantry divisions, commanded by SS-Obergruppenführer Erich von dem Bach-Zelewski, commenced a systematic sweep of the swamps.

Victims perish inside a pre-prepared pit.

Executions were generally carried out by the mass shootings of rounded-up communities, and, in some instances, the far less tidy driving of people into the swamps where in theory they would drown. To ensure the total removal of any evidence of the victims' existence, whole villages were razed: Starazhowtsy, Kremna, Dvarets, Azyarany, Khochan.

The SS Cavalry Brigade was commanded by SS-Gruppenführer und Generalleutnant Hans Otto Georg Hermann Fegelein, Eva Braun's brother-in-law by marriage to her sister, Gretl. Notwithstanding this privileged status, Fegelein was a Waffen-SS zealot, having commanded the SS Totenkopf Reiterstandarte (Horse Regiment) after the invasion of Poland at the outbreak of the Second World War in 1939. From the outset, he plunged headlong into Hitler's *Intelligenzaktion*, the often-clandestine genocide of Poland's élite: intelligentsia, teachers, priests, doctors, aristocrats. More than 100,000 selected Poles were liquidated by shooting.

By the spring of 1941, however, Fegelein's propensity for 'murder motivated by greed' attracted the first of several military inquiries into his activities which, even by Waffen-SS standards, were increasingly questionable. The pilfering of cash and luxury goods from his personal victims for repatriation to Germany brought about court martial charges. Himmler ensured that the charges were dismissed, and posted his protégé to team up with Bach-Zelewski, on 28 July, in their new headquarters at Liakhovichi in Belorussia. The brief was simple: sanitize the region of Jews and partisans, and 'drive away' women and children. Fegelein would become the first Nazi in the Holocaust to murder entire Jewish communities.

With the closing of the operation at the end of August, Fegelein reported having eliminated 14,178 Jews, 1,001 Partisans and 699 Soviet troops. Pots-war estimates put the figure much higher at 23,700 Jews killed.

On 21 September 1941, the eve of the Jewish New Year, Rosh Hashanah, a mobile killing squad entered Ejszyszki (Eišiškės), a small border town in what is now Lithuania, known in Yiddish as Eishyshok. More than 1,000 from neighbouring villages, such as Olkeniki, were translocated to Ejszyszki to facilitate the expedient, systematic eradication process.

The killing-squad members herded 3,500 Jews from the town and the surrounding region into three synagogues, where they were held for two days without food or water. Then, in two days of killing, Jewish men, women and children were taken to cemeteries, where they were stripped naked, lined up in front of open pits, and shot to death.

In 1988, when visiting the town, Yaffa Eliach, a 4-year-old Jewish girl in Ejszyszki at the time when the Nazis arrived, said, 'The Jews had died a double

The Chief of the Security Police and the SD Berlin
July 16, 1941
Einsatzgruppe A
Location: Riga
EK 1b
Location: Daugavpils

Daugavpils was occupied by the German troops on July 6. The greater part of the town was burned down during the following 2–3 days. Only a relatively small part of the town was damaged through direct fighting. The fires on the days that followed were caused by arson. Before leaving the town, the Russians released a proclamation in which they ordered the town to be burned. The Jews are said to have participated in the burnings. 5 Jews were caught red-handed during the first 3 days and were immediately shot.

The population, with the exception of a very few, had fled from the town. At present, there are approximately 8,000 persons in town again. The steady flow of returning inhabitants can be observed.

The Latvians, including the leading activists, have been, so far, absolutely passive in their anti-Semitic attitudes, not daring to take action against Jews. Until now, Dunaburg had about 45,000 inhabitants, 50% of whom were Jews. They ruled the town absolutely. As the Russians left, the Jews spread the rumour that the Russians would return soon. Thus, unlike the Lithuanians who had an active attitude, the Latvians are hesitatingly organizing and forming a front against the Jews. The Latvian population has been further weakened as the Russians, during the last fourteen days before the war's outbreak, deported about 500 Latvian families belonging to the intelligentsia to Central Russia.

Owing to the initiative of the EK [Einsatzkommando], the auxiliary police force at present consists of 240 men and has been strictly organized. New men are currently being enlisted. They help the EK as auxiliary police and are on duty in the 6 police districts established so far. Some members have been assigned to criminal police and security police work.

By July 7 the Latvians arrested 1,125 Jews, 32 political prisoners, 85 Russian workers, and 2 women criminals, the greater part during the last days. This is due to the EK backing the Latvians. Actions against the Jews are going on in an ever-increasing number. Conforming to a suggestion of the EK, the

Jews are being evacuated by the auxiliary police force from all houses still standing. The apartments are being allocated to non-Jewish inhabitants. The Jewish families are being driven out of town by the Latvians; most of the men have been arrested.

The arrested Jewish men are shot without ceremony and interred in previously prepared graves. Until now the EK 1b has shot 1,150 Jews in Daugavpils.

In Riga, Einsatzkommando 2 sifted through the entire documentary materials, searched all offices, and arrested the leading Communists as far as they could be found. These actions initiated against the Jews were headed by SS-Sturmbannführer Barth and were carried out in an exemplary manner. At present, 600 Communists and 2,000 Jews are under arrest. 400 Jews were killed during pogroms in Riga, since the arrival of EK 2, 300 by the Latvian auxiliary police and partly by our units. The prisons will be emptied completely during the next few days. Outside of Riga, within Latvia, an additional 1,600 Jews were liquidated by EK 2.

Kneeling on the edge of a trench, causing the victims to topple forward when shot from behind.

The Chief of the Security Police and the SD Berlin
Operational Situation Report USSR. No. 86
Einsatzgruppe C
Location: Novo-Ukrainka

Operations

266 Jews were liquidated as further reprisal measures against the rebellion of the Zhitomir Jews. They even sabotaged the black-out regulations at night and lit up their windows during Russian air raids.

160 persons were shot in Korosten; during the course of the actions 68 persons were executed in Byelatserkiev and 109 in Tarashcha, mostly Jews.

Thus the Sonderkommando 4a has exterminated 6,584 Bolsheviks, Jews, and asocial elements. In two cases, ethnic Germans had to be arrested. They were active in the Communist sense, participating actively in the preparations for the deportation of ethnic Germans and Ukrainians. The investigations against these have not yet been concluded.

For the time being, Einsatzkommando 5 has been divided into platoons covering a larger territory, and is systematically combing the villages of this area. Among others, several Bolshevik mayors and kolkhoz representatives were taken care of.

Besides that, several mentally retarded persons who were ordered to blow up bridges and railroad tracks and to carry out other acts of sabotage, were rendered harmless. It seems that the NKVD favoured mentally retarded persons in allocating these kind of tasks; they, in spite of their inferiority, mustered enough energy for their criminal activities. Four executions were carried out in Ulianove, 18 in Uledovka.

It was possible to take care of 229 Jews in the clean-up action carried out in Khmielnil. As a result, this area, which suffered especially from Jewish terror, is extensively cleaned up. The reaction of the population here to their deliverance from the Jews was so strong that it resulted in a Thanksgiving service.

Einsatzkommando 5 took care of 506 Bolsheviks and Jews in the course of 14 days.

In the south of the Einsatzgruppen area, there still exists an empty area with respect to security police work because military operations do not take place sufficiently far away. So far, the return of the fugitives has not started in sufficient measure. Therefore, the number of actions naturally increases in the area which lies further back [from the front],

The remaining units of Einsatzkommando 6 shot about 600 Jews in Vinnitsa.

In Krivoy-Rog, 39 officials, 11 saboteurs and looters, and 105 Jews were taken care of.

Several actions for the seizure of officials, terrorists, and migrating Jews were carried out by the Einsatzgruppen HQ in Novo-Ukrainka and vicinity. Among others, a caravan of Jews, which was taking along a wagon of loot, was stopped. The Jews were shot and the goods distributed to the population. It was possible to find and to take care of two leading Communists during a night action in Zlinka. On the basis of individual reports and of road blocks on the streets in the course of official travels, several Jews or Bolshevik agents were shot.

The office of the Higher SS and Police Leader took care of a total of 511 Jews in actions in Pilva and Stara-Sieninva.

death' – first physically, and then when their memory was erased. The Jewish cemeteries had been levelled, and headstones crushed to be used to pave roads. All that remains of the mass grave is a simple sign bearing the inscription: 'Victims of Fascism, 1941–1944'. Today, there are no Jews among the citizens of Ejszyszki.

Within days of the German army capturing Kiev in the Ukraine, on 19 September 1941 several buildings occupied by the German military were blown up by the Soviet NKVD, precipitating immediate retaliation as the Germans embarked on a pogrom to kill all the Jews of the city. An order, in both Russian and Ukrainian, was posted throughout the city: 'Kikes of the city of Kiev and vicinity! On Monday, September 29, you are to appear by 7:00 A.M. with your possessions, money, documents, valuables and warm clothing at Dorogozhitshaya Street, next to the Jewish cemetery. Failure to appear is punishable by death.'

Over the next two days, elements of the Einsatzgruppen death squads performed an act of mass slaughter unprecedented in its scope – even by Nazi standards. More than 33,000 Jewish men, women and children were brutally murdered by shooting in a ravine known as Babi Yar, in northwestern Kiev.

Mass extermination at Wielka Piaśnica, northern Poland, in which Einsatzkommando 16, commanded by the chief of the Gdańsk Gestapo, SS-Obersturmbannführer Rudolf Tröger, was a principal player.

Meeting at Rear Headquarters, Army Group South, on 26 September Major General Kurt Eberhard, the military governor, and SS-Obergruppenführer Friedrich Jeckeln, the SS and Police Leader, made the decision to annihilate the whole Jewish population of Kiev. SS-Brigadeführer Dr Otto Rasch, commander of Einsatzgruppe C, and SS-Standartenführer Paul Blobel, commander of Einsatzkommando 4a of Einsatzgruppe C, were also present. The task would be theirs.

Aided by Ukrainian collaborators, large groups of rounded-up Jews were moved to the Jewish cemetery, from where the victims were taken to Babi Yar. Here, they stripped naked before being led to the ravine, where they were forced to lie down and shot in the back of the head. A truck driver at the scene described what he saw: 'I watched what happened when the Jews – men, women and children – arrived. The Ukrainians led them past a number of different places where one after another they had to remove their luggage, then their coats, shoes, and overgarments and also underwear. They had to leave their valuables in a designated place. There was a special pile for each article of clothing. It all happened very quickly ... I don't think it was even a minute from the time each Jew took off his coat before he was standing there completely naked ...

'Once undressed, the Jews were led into the ravine which was about 150 metres long and 30 metres wide and a good 15 metres deep ... When they reached the bottom of the ravine they were seized by members of the Schultpolizei and made to lie down on top of Jews who had already been shot. That all happened very quickly. The corpses were literally in layers. A police marksman came along and shot each Jew in the neck with a submachine gun ... I saw these marksmen stand on layers of corpses and shoot one after the other ... The marksman would walk across the bodies of the executed Jews to the next Jew who had meanwhile lain down and shoot him.'

All told, 33,771 Jews were murdered at Babi Yar. Over the following months, the execution site remained in use for the shooting of gypsies and Soviet prisoners of war. Unsubstantiated Soviet accounts after the war mention 100,000 dead – the true figure will most likely never be known.

In his description of the massacre at Babi Yar, the late America-Jewish historian, Abram Sachar, speaks of the site where 'men, women, and children were systematically machine-gunned in a two-day orgy of execution. In subsequent months, most of the remaining population was exterminated ... The Jews in their thousands, with such pathetic belongings as they could carry, were herded into barbed-wire areas at the top of the ravine, guarded by Ukrainian collaborators. There they were stripped of their clothes and beaten, then led in irregular squads

Einsatzgruppe personnel in Zdołbunów county, Poland, shooting naked women and children from the Mizocz ghetto. (Photo Gustav Hille)

down the side of the ravine. The first groups were forced to lie on the ground, face down, and were machine-gunned by the Germans who kept up a steady volley.

The riddled bodies were covered with thin layers of earth and the next groups were ordered to lie over them, to be similarly dispatched. To carry out the murder of 34,000 human beings in the space of two days could not assure that all the victims had died. Hence there were a few who survived and, though badly wounded, managed to crawl from under the corpses and seek a hiding place'. A pitiful twenty-nine survived the slaughter.

In March 1942, SS-Standartenführer Paul Blobel was placed in command of Sonderaktion 1005 (Special Action 1005), or *enterdungaktion* (exhumation action), tasked with removing all evidence that people had been murdered by the Germans in *Aktion Reinhard* in occupied Poland. Prisoners from local concentration camps were employed to exhume mass graves and burn the remains of the murdered. These work groups were known as *leichenkommandos*, or 'corpse units', and were all constituent elements of Sonderkommando 1005. The commencement of the operation, however, was delayed by the assassination of Reinhard Heydrich in June that year.

In August 1943, with the Red Army offensive pushing the Germans back to the west, the Nazis dug up the bodies from the mass graves of Babi Yar and burned

German soldiers sift through enormous piles of clothing and personal of the murdered, in search of anything of value.

them in an attempt to remove the evidence of mass murder. Paul Blobel, the commander of Sonderkommando 4a, whose troops had slaughtered the Jews of Kiev, returned to Babi Yar. For more than a month, his men and workers drafted from nearby Syrets concentration camp dug up the bodies. Bulldozers were employed to uncover the burial mounds. Industrial crushers were used at the site to break down bones before incineration. The bodies were stacked on wooden logs, doused with petrol and lit. Afterwards, the members of the *leichenkommandos* were killed to ensure that no witnesses to the murders remained. However, fifteen survived to tell what had happened.

After the war, efforts to suppress the legacy failed as the Soviet media and official reports increasingly uncovered and made public the atrocities that had occurred at Babi Yar. In 1947, Soviet writer Ilya Ehrenburg, in his novel *Burya* (The Storm), dramatically described the mass murder of Kiev's Jews at Babi Yar. Preparations also commenced for the erection of a memorial at Babi Yar to the victims of Nazi genocide.

However, with the spread of Jewish nationalism through eastern Europe and after the Russian anti-Semitic campaign of 1948, determined efforts were made to erase the events of Babi Yar from the Jewish psyche that was contributing to the resurgence in Jewish fundamentalism. Even after Stalin's death in 1953, Babi Yar remained concealed in the archives of history.

Jewish intellectuals, however, would not be silenced. In October 1959, Russian writer, journalist and editor Viktor Nekrasov, became the first – in the weekly Soviet newspaper *Literaturnaya Gazeta* – to publicly demand that a monument be erected at Babi Yar.

Of far greater impact was the poem 'Babi Yar' written by Soviet and Russian poet, novelist, essayist, dramatist, screenwriter, publisher, actor, editor and director of several films, Yevgeny Yevtushenko. Openly attacking anti-Semitism, the poem, published on 19 September 1961, had a profound effect on international public opinion and Soviet youth of the time:

Wild grasses rustle over Babi Yar,
The trees look sternly, as if passing judgement.
Here, silently, all screams, and, hat in hand,
I feel my hair changing shade to grey.

And I myself, like one long soundless scream
Above the thousands of thousands interred,
I'm every old man executed here,
As I am every child murdered here.

Babi Yar Menorah Memorial, Kiev. (Photo Alex Long)

Yevtushenko was lambasted by numerous literary apologists of the Soviet state, and then by Premier Nikita Khrushchev in March 1963. The very nature of such a Jewish martyrdom was anathema to many of the regime, but the emotive timbre of Babi Yar persisted. However, it was only after the collapse of the Soviet Union in December 1991 that the new Ukrainian order accepted the uniquely Jewish sanctity of the site and an appropriate rededication organized. Three months earlier, the iconic Menorah-shaped memorial to the 100,000 Jews massacred at Babi Yar was opened on 29 September, half a century after the first mass murder of the Jews by the Einsatzgruppen at Babi Yar.

Since the fourteenth century, concentrations of Jews had been domiciled in what would become the Baltic States, concentrated in such cities as Daugavpils, Vilnius and Riga.

In a census conducted in Latvia in the mid-1930s, there were 93,479 Jews living in the country. An estimated 70,000 would be exterminated by the German occupiers, mainly at the hands of the death squads of Einsatzgruppe A, aided in their work by local collaborators, such as the Latvian Pērkonkrusts Arajs Kommando. Such was the finality and efficiency of the pogrom, that the majority of the families ceased to exist, leaving no one to mourn or attest to the events of 1941.

Between July and October 1941, the Einsatzgruppe, commanded by SS-Brigadeführer und Generalmajor der Polizei Dr Franz Walter Stahlecker, first focused the 'final solution' on the rural population of Latvia.

The Chief of the Security Police and the Security Service Berlin,
October 7, 1941
Operational Situation Report USSR No. 106

Einsatzgruppe B
Location: Smolensk
It can be observed that, just as before, the population in the area of our activities abstains from any self-defence action against the Jews. True, the population reports uniformly about the Jewish terror against them during the Soviet rule. They also complain to the German offices about new attacks from the side of the Jews (like unauthorized return from the ghetto to their previous homes, or hostile remarks against the Germans made by Jews). However, in spite of our energetic attempts, they are not ready for any action against the Jews.

Einsatzgruppe C
Location: Kiev
As a result of destruction, especially of houses, and the forced order to evacuate endangered streets, about 23,000 persons became homeless and were forced to spend the first days of the occupation in the open. They accepted this inconvenience quietly and did not cause panic.

Meanwhile, locked and empty apartments, insofar as they had not been burned and damaged, were put at the disposal of the population. A corresponding number of apartments have also become available through liquidation, thus far around 36,000 Jews on September 29 and 30, 1941.

In agreement with the city military command, all the Jews of Kiev were ordered to appear at a certain place on Monday, September 29, by 6 o'clock. This order was publicized by posters all over the town by members of the newly organized Ukrainian militia. At the same time, oral information was passed that all the Jews of Kiev would be moved to another place. In cooperation with the HQ of EG [Einsatzgruppe] C and two Kommandos of the police regiment South, Sonderkommando 4a executed 33,771 Jews on September 29 and 30. The action was carried out smoothly and no incidents occurred. The population agreed with the plan to move the Jews to another place. That they were actually liquidated has hardly been made known. However, according to the experience gained so far, this would not meet with any opposition. The army has also approved the measures taken.

The Militia headquarters, according to a suggestion of Sonderkommando 4a, arranged a temporary, local concentration of Jews in Zhitmmir. This resulted in a quieter atmosphere, for example, in the markets, etc. At the same time, obstinate rumours diminished, and it seemed that together with the concentration of the Jews, the Communists, too, lost much ground. However, it became obvious after a few days that concentration of the Jews without building a ghetto did not suffice, and that the old difficulties emerged again after a short while. Complaints about the impertinence of the Jews in their various places of work stemmed from various quarters.

Therefore, a conference was called together with military H.Q. on September 10, 1941. The resulting decision was the final and radical liquidation of the Jews of Zhitomir, since all warnings and special measures had not led to any perceptible change.

On September 19, 1941, from 4 o'clock [a.m.], the Jewish quarter was emptied after having been surrounded and closed the previous evening by 60 members of the Ukrainian militia. The transport was accomplished in 12 trucks, part of which had been supplied by military headquarters and part by the city administration of Zhitomir. After the transport had been carried out and the necessary preparations made with the help of 150 prisoners, 3,145 Jews were registered and shot.

Valuables and money were conveyed to the Sonderkommando 4a.

In mid-August, the Jews of Riga, the capital of Latvia, were ordered into a ghetto established in the city's impoverished Moscow quarter. Weeks later, the ghetto was sealed off, imprisoning 29,602 Jews: 8,212 men, 15,738 women and 5,652 children. On 30 November, a fleet of new, blue Riga motor-buses began an orderly ferrying of ghetto inhabitants to a remote forest spot not far from the railhead at Rumbula.

The Rumbula massacre refers to incidents on two non-consecutive days – 30 November and 8 December 1941 – during which some 25,000 Jews were murdered in or on the way to Rumbula forest. Apart from the Babi Yar massacre, this was the biggest two-day Holocaust atrocity prior to the introduction of the death camps. Of this number, approximately 24,000 were Jews from the Riga ghetto, and 1,000 German Jews transported to the forest by train.

The Rumbula massacre was carried out by Einsatzgruppe A with the help of local collaborators of the Arajs Kommando, with support from other such

Execution of members of the National Liberation Front, Stari Pisker, Slovenia, July 1942

Latvian auxiliaries. Placed in charge of the Rumbula operation was 46-year-old SS-Obergruppenführer Friedrich Jeckeln, who had previously overseen similar massacres in Ukraine, including Babi Yar.

At Rumbula, Jeckeln personally watched on both days as 25,000 Jews were slaughtered in his presence. Jeckeln proved to be a cold, automated butcher, who, unfaltering, exterminated large numbers of vulnerable, defenceless, naked men, women and children. Frida Michelson was one of only three who miraculously survived Rumbula, by feigning death as the next batches of victims covered her with their footwear: 'A mountain of footwear was pressing down on me. My body was numb from cold and immobility. However, I was fully conscious now. The snow under me had melted from the heat of my body. Quiet for a while. Then from the direction of the trench a child's cry: "Mama! Mama! Mamaa!" A few shots. Quiet. Killed.'

By the end of August 1941, while commanding the SS First Brigade in western Ukraine, Jeckeln had personally directed the killing of more than 44,000 Jews, the largest total that month. The combined killing *aktions* constitute one of the largest death tolls during the Einsatzgruppen period of 'holocaust by bullets'.

On 27 January 1942, Jeckeln was awarded the War Merit Cross with Swords for liquidating the 25,000 at Rumbula on orders from the top.

Soviet memorial to the victims, among other citizens of Riga, of the Rumbula Forest massacre. (Photo M. Striķis)

Simferopol, a city in the Crimea, was founded in 1784, where Crimean Jews, or Krymchaks, from elsewhere in the Crimea and Ashkenazi Jews from the Pale of Settlement began to settle. During the nineteenth century, the Jewish population increased considerably, and by 1897, the Jews numbered 8,950, or 18 per cent of the city's population.

In October 1905, pogroms were conducted in the city in which forty-two Jews were murdered. The First World War and the Civil War years witnessed many Jews finding refuge in Simferopol. The city became an important Zionist centre for helping Russian emigrants to Palestine. Jews in the city numbered 22,800 in 1939, or 16 per cent of the total population. Simferopol fell to the Germans on 1 November 1941, where they found some 12,000–14,000 Jews.

Einsatzgruppen D's Sonderkommando 10b followed shortly behind the Wehrmacht, and by 13 December 1941 had eradicated more than 10,000 Jews and some 2,500 Krymchaks.

The Chief of the Security Police and Security Service Berlin
November 2, 1941
Operational Situation Report USSR No. 128
Einsatzgruppe C
Location: Kiev

As to purely execution matters, approximately 80,000 persons have been liquidated by now by the Kommandos of the Einsatzgruppe. Among these are approximately 8,000 persons convicted after investigation of anti-German or Bolshevist activities. The remainder was liquidated in retaliatory actions. Several measures were carried out as large-scale actions. The largest of these took place immediately after the occupation of Kiev. It was carried out exclusively against Jews and their families.

The difficulties resulting from such a large-scale action, in particular concerning the round-up, were overcome in Kiev by requesting the Jewish population to assemble, using wall posters. Although at first only the participation of 5–6,000 Jews had been expected, more than 30,000 Jews arrived who, until the moment of their execution, still believed in their resettlement, thanks to extremely clever organization.

Even though approximately 75,000 Jews have been liquidated in this manner, it is evident at this time that this cannot be the best solution of the Jewish problem. Although we succeeded, particularly in smaller towns and villages, in bringing about a complete liquidation of the Jewish problem, nevertheless, again and again it has been observed in the larger cities that after such an action, all Jews have indeed been eradicated. But, when after a certain period of time a Kommando returns, the number of Jews still found in the city always surpasses considerably the number of executed Jews.

Besides, the Kommandos have also carried out military actions in numerous cases. On request of the Army, separate platoons of the Kommandos have repeatedly combed the woods searching for partisans, and have accomplished successful work there.

Finally, it should be mentioned that prisoners-of-war were taken over from the prisoner assembly points and the prisoner-of-war transit camps, although at times, considerable disagreements with the camp commander occurred.

Raid by German field gendarmes and soldiers in Simferopol, January 1942. (Photo Bundesarchiv)

At the beginning of November, SS-Gruppenführer und Generalleutnant der Polizei Dr Otto Ohlendorf, commander of Einsatzgruppe D, transferred the staff of his unit from Nikolayev to Simferopol, the Crimean capital. The city, in what remains the disputed Crimean Peninsula, was an important German garrison and logistics base, including the staffs of the XXX and LIV army corps, the 72nd and 22nd infantry divisions, the Head Quarter Master, and the commander of the Luftwaffe at 11th Army.

The Ortskommandantur, or Local Command Post I/853, under a certain Captain Kleiner, was in charge of the city's administration, whose function was also to conduct a census of the local population, based on ethnic origins. Kleiner's survey revealed that, of the original 156,000 inhabitants, 120,000 of various population groups still remained in Simferopol, including 11,000 of the 20,000 pre-occupation Jews. Kleiner's report of 14 November 1941 – now kept in the German Federal Archives, Bundesarchiv – confidently declared that these Jews would be 'executed by the SD'.

However, the implementation of this pogrom in Simferopol presented a conundrum, resulting in a delay of several weeks. The issues of ethnic ideologies and practicality of implementation had to be addressed. Ideologically, in the Crimean

Peninsula, there were three disparate population groups that, theoretically, conformed with Nazi policies regarding the classification of Jews:

1. The Karaim, an ethnic group derived from Turkic-speaking adherents of Karaite Judaism in Central and Eastern Europe, of whom SS-Obergruppenführer Gottlob Berger wrote: 'Their Mosaic religion is unwelcome. However, on grounds of race, language and religious dogma ... discrimination against the Karaites is unacceptable.'
2. The Krymchaks, Jewish ethno-religious communities of the Crimea derived from Turkic-speaking adherents of Orthodox Judaism.
3. Ashkenazi Jews, a Jewish diaspora population who amalgamated as a distinct community during the Holy Roman Empire in the first millennium. The traditional diaspora language of Ashkenazi Jews is Yiddish, a Germanic language which incorporates several dialects.

Whilst there was no question that the Ashkenazi group should be liquidated, uncertainty prevailed among Nazi policymakers about how to address the

Mass shooting of Serbian partisans and their supporters.

The Chief of the Security Police and the Security Service Berlin
November 12, 1941
Operational Situation Report USSR NO. 132
Einsatzgruppe C
Dniepropetrovsk

The number of executions carried out by Sonderkommando 4a has meanwhile increased to 55,432.

Among those executed by Sonderkommando 4a in the latter half of October 1941 until the date of this report, in addition to a comparatively small number of political functionaries, active Communists, people guilty of sabotage, etc., the larger part were again Jews. A considerable part of these were Jewish prisoners-of-war handed over by the German Army at Borispol, at the request of the Commander of the Borispol POW camp. On October 14, 1941 a platoon of Sonderkommando 4a shot 752 Jewish prisoners-of-war, among them some commissars and 78 wounded Jews handed over by the camp physician.

Another platoon of Sonderkommando 4a was active at Lubny. Without any opposition, it executed 1,363 Jews, Communists, and partisans, among them 53 prisoners-of-war and a few Jewish rifle-women. Before the war, Lubny had 35,000 inhabitants, among them 14,000 Jews. A recent census undertaken by the local municipal administration showed that of 20,000 inhabitants allegedly only 1,500 Jews can be listed.

Sonderkommando 4b is stationed in Poltava, according to a report dated October 16, 1941. Slaviansk is to be its next location. The work of Sonderkommando 4b, influenced partly by weather and road conditions, was mainly limited to the area of Poltava. In the week from October 4, 1941 to October 10, 1941, a total of 186 persons were executed, among them 21 political functionaries, four people guilty of sabotage and looting, and 161 Jews. In addition, the task of the Sonderkommando included searches and pursuits of former leading Communist functionaries and members of the executive committee of the Poltava district.

The number of people executed by Einsatzkommando 5 amounted to 15,110 on October 20, 1941. Of this number, 20 political functionaries, 21 people guilty of sabotage and looting, and 1,847 Jews were shot between October 13, 1941 and October 19, 1941. On October 18, 1941, 300 insane Jews from the Kiev lunatic asylum were liquidated. This represented a particularly heavy psychological burden for the members of Einsatzkommando 5 who were in charge of this operation.

A large part of the work of Einsatzkommando 5 is dealing with denunciations which are reported daily in great numbers by all classes of the population. These necessitate subsequent interrogations and investigations.

Between September 23, 1941 and October 4, 1941, 85 political functionaries, 14 people guilty of sabotage and looting, and 179 Jews were executed in Dniepropetrovsk.

---

other two groups. After consulting his experts on racial issues, Himmler himself – who had asserted that it was his prerogative to decide who was and who was not Jewish – eventually decided that the Karaim would be spared the bullet, as, racially, they were not Jewish. The Krymchaks, however, were racially categorized with the Ashkenazi to be killed. Himmler's decision would have been made between 5 December 1941, when he still made written references to the 'Krymchak issue' and 9 December 1941, the day on which the Krymchaks of Simferopol were murdered. The practical dilemma facing the *Aktion* operations against Simferopol's Jews in November 1941, was the incessant problems posed by Soviet partisan activity on the peninsula. Embellished Wehrmacht reports about partisan strengths and successes forced the supreme command of the 11th Army, designated Kommandostab München, to commit all its resources into fighting the partisans, while Einsatzgruppe D was employed on reconnaissance duty on partisan movements.

Early in December, the partisan threat diminished significantly after around 1,000 partisans had been killed or captured. With the arrival of the 1st and 4th Romanian 'Vanatori de Munte' mountain brigades in the Crimea as reinforcement to the Wehrmacht, SS-Gruppenführer und Generalleutnant der Polizei Dr Otto Ohlendorf could now withdraw his men from anti-partisan reconnaissance duty. At this time, the Einsatzkommando 11b, commanded by SS-Obersturmbannführer Werner Braune, was also transferred from Odessa to Simferopol, thereby providing Ohlendorf with the additional resources to expedite his prime task of annihilating the Jews.

Simferopol Wehrmacht Head Quarter Master Colonel Friedrich-Wilhelm Hauck saw the immediate elimination of the Jews as an excellent way ease the

Damaged German vehicle in the aftermath of a partisan attack, Simferopol, c. December 1941. (Photo Bundesarchiv)

critical food situation in the city by getting rid of superfluous mouths to feed. The 11th Army commander, Generaloberst Erich von Manstein fully endorsed the pogrom with an order he issued on 20 November 1941, in which he stated: 'For the need of visiting harsh atonement on Jewry, the spiritual carrier of Bolshevism, the soldier must show understanding. It is also necessary in order to choke at birth all revolts, which are mostly incited by Jews.'

On 9 December 1941, von Manstein's desire for 'atonement' materialized when Sonderkommando 11b and the staff of Einsatzgruppe D eradicated the city's Krymchaks, numbering at least 1,500 Jews. Quite unexpectedly, the *aktion* was then halted for two days when Ohlendorf was faced with a problem in the ranks: men of the 4th Company, Police Reserve Battalion 9, who had assisted Einsatzgruppe D in its pogroms since the start of the Soviet campaign, declared that they had had enough of all the mindless slaughter, and were requesting transfer to other duties. Ohlendorf acquiesced, so he had to wait for the arrival at Simferopol for a replacement unit, the 3rd Company, Police Reserve Battalion 3.

For the 3rd Company, there was no acclimatization or introduction into their grisly new task. They were unceremoniously plunged into the bloodbath where, with the assistance of elements from detachments of Einsatzgruppe D, both police

Slovenian partisan Franc Sešek about to be shot.

battalions, the detached members of Feldgendarmerie Abteilung (Field Military Police), or FGA 683, the Geheime Feldpolizei (Secret Field Police), or GFP 647, Braune's Sonderkommando 11b, and Ohlendorf's staff of Einsatzgruppe D, the mass murder of Simferopol Jews recommenced on 11 December. Braune simply informed the diverse conglomerate that they would be participating in a *grosskampftag*, a major combat day. The medics would be required to go along.

The slaughter of the Jews lasted for three days. The victims were required to gather at the former Communist Party building in the city centre. There, they were instructed to hand over all their personal belongings, including valuables, on the premise that this was for the safekeeping of their property while en route to perform labour duties. They would be handed back on their return.

Einsatzgruppe and heavy army vehicles, public buses and a miscellany of small trucks and vans rapidly transported the wary Jews to an anti-tank ditch on the outskirts of Simferopol. Caught totally unawares, the 3rd Police Reserve Battalion Company immediately received orders to use their weapons to murder. Many quickly realized why their colleagues from Police Reserve Battalion 9 had succumbed mentally to the sheer and repugnant task they themselves were now performing.

Under the watchful gaze of both Ohlendorf and Braune, over and over the killing command rang out to lines of fifty men firing in unison: 'Ready, aim, fire!' The more experienced members of the Einsatzgruppe would then, in between salvos, trample over the dead and dying in the pit to deliver the coup de grâce wherever they encountered life. Army troops also took part in the shooting, but it remains unclear if these were exclusively military policemen and members of the Geheime Feldpolizei, or from the Wehrmacht's general rank and file.

In the bitterly cold winter's day, other preselected prisoners were tasked with piling up the corpses in the ditch and filling spaces. Bodies that had not fallen in when shot also had to be dragged and dumped into the rapidly filling pit.

Those who tried to escape or feign death were shot by members of the Einsatzgruppe armed with sub-machine guns. In some cases, with cold cynicism, decisions were made not to waste any further ammunition on a victim still alive in the pit as the earth thrown over the corpses would suffocate them anyway. In one instance, a young Jew who had offered resistance was ordered beaten to death rather than shot.

As the days passed and the numbers of Jews arriving for execution started to fall off, the Einsatzgruppe extended its net to include Simferopol's gypsies. Presumably, a request had been made by the German administration or the Wehrmacht that led to the decision to also liquidate this population group.

A young partisan is captured. He will undoubtedly be shot or hanged. (Photo Bundesarchiv)

In the Operational Situation Report, USSR No. 150 of 2 January 1942, Ohlendorf reported that, with the end of the *aktion* on 15 December 1941, Simferopol, along with other parts of the Crimea, had been made free of Jews. Many Jews, however, remained in hiding. Smaller pogroms throughout the Crimea continued until the end of the year.

At the war crimes trial of Generalfeldmarschall Erich von Manstein in Hamburg from 23 August to 19 December 1949, his defence counsel, English solicitor Reginald T. Paget, fought to have his client exonerated of any complicit involvement in the Crimean massacres, especially the mass murder at Simferopol. Contending that the reports of the atrocities was an orchestrated instrument of Soviet propaganda, Paget vehemently contested the veracity of the events at Simferopol:

To me, the numbers stated by the SD appeared to be entirely impossible. Individual companies of about 100 men with about 8 vehicles are declared to have killed 10,000 to 12,000 Jews in two or three days. Since, as one will recall, the Jews believed in a resettlement and consequently took their belongings along with them, the SD could not possibly have transported more than twenty or thirty Jews respectively in one truck. For each vehicle, with loading, 10 km of driving, unloading and return, an estimated two hours had to elapse. The Russian winter day is short and there was no night driving. In order to kill 10,000 Jews, at least three weeks would have been necessary.

In one case we were able to check the numbers. The SD claimed to have killed 10,000 Jews in Simferopol in November and declared the city free of Jews in December. Through a series of counter-tests, we were able to prove that the shooting of Jews in Simferopol had taken place on a single day, namely on November 16. There was only a single SD company in Simferopol. The place for the execution was situated 15km away from the city. The number of victims could not have been greater than 300, and these 300 were in all probability not only Jews, but a collection of different elements who were under suspicion of belonging to the resistance movement.

The Simferopol affair leaked out at the time of the trial to broad strata of the public, since it was being mentioned by the sole living witness to the charge, an Austrian private by the name of Gaffal. He claimed that he had heard the Jewish operation mentioned in a sappers' mess, where he was the ordnance man, and that he had passed by the place of execution near Simferopol. After this testimony we received a quantity of letters and were able to produce several witnesses who had stayed near Jewish families in the Quarter and reported about the religious services in the synagogue as well as a Jewish market, where they bought icons and junk goods – up to the time of Manstein's departure from the Crimea and afterwards. There was no doubt at all that the Jewish community in Simferopol had continued to exist openly, and although some of our opponents had heard rumours of violence by the SD against the Jews in Simferopol, it nevertheless appeared that the Jewish community was unaware of any particular danger.

Of the nine charges against von Manstein, he was found not guilty on the three charges relating to the liquidation of Jews. A prison sentence of eighteen years was handed down, later reduced to twelve. He was released from prison in May 1953, and died in June 1973. Von Manstein may not have personally pulled the trigger, but in his capacity as a top Wehrmacht officer, he did nothing to nothing to prevent the mass slaughter of innocent men, women and children.

During the night of 23–24 October 1941, the Ukrainian city of Kharkov (Kharkiv) fell to the Wehrmacht's LV Army Corps, commanded by General der Infanterie Erwin Vierow. Due to its northeastern proximity to the Soviet front, Kharkov was not incorporated into the Reichskommissariat Ukraine, and the role of occupying authority was vested in the staff of the corps. Generalmajor Anton Dostler,

Erich von Manstein greets Adolf Hitler on the Eastern Front. (Photo Bundesarchiv)

The Chief of the Security Police and Security Service Berlin
November 21, 1941
Operational Situation Report USSR No. 136

Activities of Einsatzgruppe A
The advance unit of Einsatzgruppe A continued their security measures and activities as security police.

As a result of an investigation in the area around Krasnoye Selo, which took place from October 18 to 28, 1941, 70 suspicious persons were arrested and thoroughly interrogated. Seven persons were convicted of being members of partisan groups and of the Communist Party, as well as for participating in acts of sabotage. They confessed and were executed. The remainder of the arrested persons was released. The provisional mayor appointed by the local military commander in Krasnoye Selo and some of his assistants were objectionable from a political point of view. With the agreement of the local military commander, they were discharged and the two of them were executed, since they had previously been active in the Communist Party. In all, 118 persons were executed in the period October 24 to November 5, 1941, 31 of these because of their activities as agents.

commander of the 57th Infantry Division, was appointed *Stadtkommandant* until 13 December. One of Dostler's first acts as head of the occupying administration, was to issue a terse and foreboding set of instructions aimed at Kharkov's residents:

1. The winner can use all means to restore and maintain law and order in Kharkov.

2. Unruly elements, saboteurs and guerrillas, who should be sought almost exclusively among the Jews, must be punished by death. Likewise, public execution by hanging should be conducted and victims should be left hung for purposes of intimidation. The executed bodies should be protected by auxiliary police. Jews, Jewish stores, and Jewish businesses should be somehow marked.

3. It is necessary and required to be extremely harsh in dealing with the inhabitants

An Einsatzgruppen method of mass murder.

Prior to the arrival on 16 November of the Sonderkommando 4A of Einsatzgruppe C, under the command of SS-Standartenführer Paul Blobel, Kharkov witnessed random hangings and shootings of partisans, communists, saboteurs and selected civilians.

The *Stadtkommandant* continued to issue decrees aimed at understanding the logistics of addressing the Jewish issue in the city: 'A registration is being conducted according to the lists of the approved format. For each building two lists must be produced: in the first list all inhabitants of the building should be recorded, with the exception of Zhids ['dirty' Jews]. In the second list all Zhids should be recorded, regardless of their religion.'

The ghetto relocation of Jews in the city commenced, with the Tractor and Machine Tool Plant barracks the designated concentration point. A prison was opened on Rybnaya Street in the garage of the Sonderkommando 4A. Only a few dozen residents, mostly Jews, were incarcerated in the makeshift facility, where they were forced into hard labour, beaten, made to stand naked in the cold while drenched with water, and were randomly shot.

Several hundred ill, infirm and elderly people, who could not make it to the plant by 16 December, were rounded up and locked in the Meshchanskaya Street synagogue where they all perished of hunger and cold.

The Chief of the Security Police and Security Service Berlin
January 5, 1942
Operational Situation Report USSR No. 151

Situation in Krasnogvardeisk and vicinity
In answer to the concrete question why some people reject Bolshevism, they give three reasons:

1) Bolshevism has, they claim, destroyed their property and taken away all their land. They claimed that they earned hardly enough for their essential needs.
2) They said that Bolshevism had destroyed religion.
3) They said that the leading persons in Bolshevism were Jews.

All the Jews, without exception, in the General Kommissariats Lithuania and Latvia, are now interned in ghettos. The Jews of the Riga ghetto who are employed by the German Army and civilian authorities, are no longer permitted to go freely to their places of work. In the morning, they are picked up in closed columns by authorized personnel who then escort them from the ghetto to their work place, and returning them in the evening the same way.

In Minsk, as well as in Riga, everything is prepared for the reception of the Jewish transports from Germany. The first transport, composed of Jews from Hamburg, arrived in Minsk on November 10, 1941. On the same day, the Jews were assigned living quarters. It was observed that some of the Jews had a totally mistaken picture about their future. They imagined, for example, that they are pioneers and will be used to colonize the East. The first three transports that were to come to Riga were sent to Kaunas. The Riga camp that is to admit about 25,000 Jews is being built and will be completed very soon.

In the meantime, the Higher SS Police in Riga, SS-Obergruppenfuhrer Jeckeln started a shooting action on Sunday, November 30, 1941. He removed about 4,000 Jews from the Riga ghetto and from an evacuation transport of Jews from Germany. The action was originally intended to be carried out with the forces of the Higher SS and Police Chief; however, after a few hours, 20 men of Einsatzkommando 2 who were sent there for security purposes were also employed in the shooting.

In fact, the action took place on November 30. Of approximately 10,600 victims, 1,000 were from a transport of deportees from Berlin, and the rest from the ghetto. The remaining Jews were killed a week later on December 8.

On 18 December, elements of Sonderkommando 4A removed 200 Jewish patients out of a psychiatric hospital, ostensibly to relocate them to the new Jewish settlement. However, they were all executed.

The annihilation of the ghetto commenced in mid-December. The Jewish victims were duped into believing that they were being transported to labour camps in Poltava. Instead, they were taken to Drobytsky Yar, a ravine near the city. Between December 1941 and January 1942, an estimated 30,000 men, women and children – half of them Jewish – were murdered and interred in a mass grave under the direction of the regional Einsatzgruppe.

In January 1942, as the bitterly cold Arctic weather disabled Eastern Europe, Hitler's war machine stalled in its conquest of the Soviet Union. In spite of this, the Jewish pogroms continued unabated.

In Belorussia, where partisan resistance against the German armies was noticeably stronger than elsewhere, Einsatzgruppe B, under SS-Brigadeführer und Generalmajor der Polizei Erich Naumann, was falling short of its quotas of liquidated Jews and communists demanded by Heydrich. This, together with the harassment by the anti-German partisans, resulted in a substantial increase in the work of the death squads. Entire villages were razed, and all their inhabitants shot.

To enhance the efficiency of the relatively small Einsatzgruppen B, additional contingents of death squads were sent to Belorussia from the Ukraine, Latvia and Lithuania. The pool from which these volunteers were drawn was largely comprised of impoverished rural peasants, who were in no position to refuse food, clothing and cash. Ignorant as to their duties, they were merely transported to the region, where they disembarked at Minsk.

As their grim actions began, they found that in most villages the men were away fighting, leaving only women, children and the elderly or very young as their selected targets.

At the mass-execution sites, parents were shot before their children, with the rationale that the adults would not see their children being shot. In sordid acts of mercy, small children were often shot to avoid suffocation from the dead falling on top of them as they were shot. Older children tended to comply with the instructions to lie down in the pits before being shot.

Elements of the Einsatzkommando would cordon off the killing ground and simply supervise the paid killers, who had been fortified with a big tot of vodka before assuming their firing positions. It was not uncommon for there to be so many of these auxiliaries, that each one only had to shoot two to three times. Upon completion, POWs or internees from nearby concentration camps would then be brought in to pour disinfectant over the bodies before covering them with soil.

A hanged partisan, Minsk.

The SS officers tended not to participate in the actual shootings, preferring instead to walk among the bodies after the shooting and administering the coup de grâce with a pistol on those who were only wounded. It was reported that the victims were generally stoical when facing imminent death.

On the morning of 27 May 1942, SS-Obergruppenführer und General der Polizei Reinhard Heydrich, acting Reichsprotektor of the Nazi Protectorate of Bohemia and Moravia (formerly part of Czechoslovakia), was being driven to his office in Prague Castle. As his staff car slowed down to navigate a corner in the suburb of Holesovice, British-trained Czech patriots, Jozef Gabčík and Jan Kubiš ambushed the car. A grenade wrecked the vehicle, leaving Heydrich badly wounded. He was rushed to Bulovka Hospital in Prague, but on 4 June, he died from septicaemia caused by scraps of upholstery and clothing entering his body when the grenade exploded.

In Berlin, Hitler was frantic with rage and, characteristically, what he demanded was not justice, but retribution. He ordered the instant execution off 30,000 Czechs as a reprisal.

Karl Hermann Frank, the Sudeten German Secretary of State – Heydrich's death had left him in command at Prague – was reticent, on the grounds that this would seriously deplete the badly needed labour force in the protectorate.

As a consequence, Hitler amended his order to the arrest of 10,000 Prague residents, and that very night, 27 May, a priority signal from Himmler reached Frank, which read: 'As the intellectuals are our main enemy, shoot 100 of them tonight.' Over the next few days, 3,188 Czechs were arrested, of whom 1,357 were executed, while 657 more died 'under police investigation'.

This was by no means adequate to satisfy Hitler. On 9 June, the day after Heydrich's funeral, Frank received a top-secret signal from Hitler, ordering him to 'carry out a special reprisal action to teach the Czechs a final lesson of subservience and humility'. He was to choose a small working-class community near an industrial centre, and remove it from the face of the planet. This sat well with Frank: his hatred of the Czechs was pathological, and he had already made a similar suggestion himself.

The name of a village called Lidice happened to be on the files, as it was from here that two men, Josef Horak and Josef Stribrny, had left Czechoslovakia in 1939 and were known to be serving in the RAF.

Berlin was demanding immediate action, and two Gestapo agents were hastily despatched to Lidice that night to arrange for the necessary 'evidence' to be discovered in the morning to incriminate the village.

The car in which Reinhard Heydrich was ambushed in Prague. (Photo Bundesarchiv)

What the people of Lidice thought of recent events in Prague was not recorded. Probably the day-to-day details of their hardworking lives absorbed most of their energies. At least, the first incursion of the Germans into their village seems to have taken them by surprise. Although German troops were not an uncommon sight at that time, there were over 100,000 of them in the protectorate and one saw them about everywhere. Lidice, however, was off the main road, and the Germans had never before come there in force.

At about 4.30 p.m. on the afternoon of 4 June, two columns of troops in lorries appeared on a rise above the village. Jumping from the vehicles, the German soldiers spread out across the fields to form a cordon, herding the apprehensive people inward until they were all collected in the main street through the village. Gestapo men in their black uniforms abruptly questioned them, assiduously identifying each individual from type-written lists.

Meanwhile, police ransacked every house from top to bottom, turning furniture and belongings upside down, and leaving a trail of chaos behind them. Then, suddenly, it ended as the Germans all climbed back into their vehicles and left. They took with them Madame Stribrny and her brother, and the whole Horak family, comprising eight men and seven women, one of whom heavily pregnant. None of them was seen again.

The stunned villagers were left to restore their shattered households as best they could. They could only speculate about what the Germans had been looking for, and whether they would return.

Five days later, on 9 June, they came back, but this time quite late in the evening. At 9.30 p.m., after many of the villagers had already retired for the night, a convoy of trucks arrived. The occupants immediately surrounded the village and set up barriers on every exit, while a string of staff cars sped into the square with groups of SS and Gestapo officers. The villagers were called out, many in their pyjamas, and made to line up in the square, men on one side, and women and children on the other. As previously, the night visitors meticulously ticked them off one by one on their tidy lists. Boys over 15 were put with the men, who were then placed under armed guard in the empty buildings of the Horak farm. The women and children were herded into the school, where all personal belongings were confiscated. Then they were locked in for the night.

At the same time, squads of Schutzpolizei were methodically ransacking the houses, collecting everything of value. The incriminating 'evidence', provided by their colleagues, was soon discovered. Cattle were rounded up and driven away, and tools and agricultural implements collected and carted off. The pillage continued through the night.

When the doors of the school were unlocked at 5 a.m. the next morning, the women came out to find their village a shambles, the street littered with the broken remains of their humble belongings. They were bundled into a row of covered trucks and driven away, not knowing where to or why. As the lorries left the village, the backs of the village men could be seen by some of the women, lined up in the courtyard of the Horak farm. It was the last that any of them would ever see of their menfolk.

The special extermination squad from Prague arrived at the village. They propped up a line of mattresses against the wall of the barn to prevent ricochets, and then they brought out the men and boys, ten at a time, lined them up, and shot them – 173 in all. From 10 a.m. in the morning until 3 p.m. that afternoon, the slaughter continued, until no living being was left alive in the village of Lidice. Even the dogs were shot in their kennels. Some of the men were not even residents of Lidice – they had merely been visiting friends that evening. Some of the village men were absent, working late shifts in mines and factories at Kladno. However, they were not overlooked. They were collected and shot later, bringing the final total of male residents massacred to 192.

The next task was to obliterate any evidence that the village of Lidice ever existed. Under the supervision of Frank himself, gangs went around with cans of petrol firing the buildings. After them came engineers with charges to blow up any walls left still standing, while bulldozers were employed to level the ruins, uproot fruit trees, and fill in the lake. They even diverted the stream. Ploughs were then driven back and forth across the acres of rubble, so that no identifiable outline remained. The sanitization complete, a high, barbed-wire fence was erected around the site, with notices in Czech and German, warning: 'Anyone approaching this fence who does not halt when challenged will be shot.' Lidice had evaporated.

The balance of the village residents – 198 women and 98 children – had been driven to Kladno, where they were shut up in the local secondary school gymnasium, where they were left for three days, without food, water or sanitation, pondering what was happening to their menfolk at home.

When they were finally let out, armed SS men informed them that issues at Lidice had been resolved and that they would now be transported to a 'distant camp'. Owing to transport difficulties, however, children under the age of 15 years had to go by bus, while the rest would go by train.

The children having been removed, the distraught women were packed into cattle trucks to commence the long slow journey to Ravensbruck concentration camp. Upon arrival, thirty-five of the older women were separated from the others and transported to the extermination camp at Auschwitz, where they were used for medical experiments. When the Soviets liberated the camp in April 1945, only six were still alive.

On 12 October 1942, in Mizocz, Ukraine, elements of the Einsatzgruppen Ordnungspolizei and Ukrainian Auxiliary Police cordoned off the Jewish ghetto in this erstwhile eastern Polish village, in preparation for the elimination of all 1,700 residents. Two days later, they were trucked out to a remote ravine, where they were told to strip and lay down on their stomachs. They were then shot one by one.

Shortly after the Einsatzgruppen commenced their operations, several commanders were becoming cognizant of the psychological impact that the mass murders were having on their men. From mid-July 1941, Einsatzgruppe A commander, SS-Brigadeführer und Generalmajor der Polizei, Dr Franz Walter Stahlecker, began reporting on widespread nervous breakdowns and associated

A bronze sculpture by Marie Uchytilova in Lidice, Czech Republic, commemorates a group of eighty-two children from Lidice who were gassed at Chełmno in the summer of 1942. (Photo Moravice)

The Chief of the Security Police and Security Service Berlin
March 6, 1942
Operational Situation Report USSR NO. 177
Einsatzgruppe C
Location: Kiev

The strong measures taken by the Einsatzgruppe against the Jews and former Communist Party members had good results with respects to the feelings of the general public. After the advance of the front had come to a standstill, the long stay of the kommandos resulted in a considerable accumulation of cases. Police activity suffered very much from the cold temperature and the obliteration of tracks by the snow.

Sonderkommando 4b executed 1,317 people (among them 63 political agitators, 30 saboteurs and partisans, and 1,224 Jews). With this action, the district of Artemovsk was also freed of Jews.

As a result of the activity of Einsatzkommando 5, a number of political agitators, 114 saboteurs and looters, as well as 1,580 Jews were shot, in all 1,880 people. This kommando also carried out an action against the Bandera group.

As a result of the measures carried out by Einsatzkommando 6, both the Gorlovka and Makeyevka districts are free now of Jews. A small number who remained in Stalino will be moved as soon as weather conditions permit. A total of 493 people were executed here, among them 80 political agitators, 44 saboteurs and looters, and 369 Jews.

The number of arrested old members of the Communist Party remaining here is striking. This suggests specific intentions of the enemy in this zone. Also, four armed parachutists were liquidated here.

alcohol addiction. Incidents had also arisen in which individuals would feign illnesses to avoid participating in the genocide. Yet others appeared to have developed an immunity to the stresses of the job, performing the slaughter like soulless automatons. The consumption of alcohol – the analgesic of choice – reached epidemic proportions. For some, the derivation of sadistic pleasure from murdering defenceless human beings fuelled them.

Long after the war, Ukrainian Kazymyr Vychnevsky spoke of the horrors to which he had been a witness. Recalling one massacre in July 1942, he said the large crowd of 7,500 Jewish victims started screaming when they saw the armed firing squads arriving. There were only a few Germans from the local Einsatzkommando – the rest were Ukrainian auxiliaries.

A young girl, perhaps only 6 years old, broke away from the milling Jews and crawled on her hands and knees through the clover. She had only reached as far as Vychnevsky's cart when a German walked over and shot her in the head.

Afterwards, it was Vychnevsky's requisitioned task, using his plough, to move the corpses of those who had tried to flee into the pit with the rest of the bodies. While awaiting instructions near the pit, he was summoned over to where elements of the death squads were lounging on the ground by their machine guns, smoking. As he approached, he could see and smell that the men were in an advanced stage of intoxication.

As Vychnevsky stood drinking the schnapps he had been given, a German came down the dirt road towards them, escorting two teenage girls, aged between 16 and eighteen. He stood them at the edge of the pit, then went to join his drinking comrades to participate in the imbibing of copious amounts of vodka and schnapps. The two petrified girls were like a couple of statues – there was nowhere to run. It was then that the German suddenly remembered the two girls. Following instructions, a member of the group picked up his rifle and staggered

Victims dig their own graves, Piaśnica, northern Poland.

over to the pit – he was paralytic. When he got there, he kicked one of the girls in her rear, causing her to tumble into water in the bottom of the pit. As she started wading away, the guard tried to shoot her, but the alcohol had rendered him incapable of seeing straight. He kept firing and missing until, through sheer luck, he found his target.

SS-Gruppenführer und Generalmajor der Polizei Arthur Nebe, commander of Einsatzgruppe B in Belorussia, would succumb to the stresses of the genocide after his chauffeur, his mind no longer able to process the carnage that filled every day of his life, took his own life. In November 1941, Nebe asked Berlin to relieve him of his position and the responsibilities and functions that went with the post. By that time, in what is today Belarus, he had liquidated 45,000 Jews. Nebe returned to his previous job in the RHSA.

After the failed attempt on Hitler's life on 20 July 1944, in which he had been involved, Nebe, in charge of a dozen policemen, prepared to assassinate Himmler. However, the signal initiating the plot never reached Nebe, and he was forced to go into hiding. After being betrayed by his mistress, Nebe was arrested on an island on the Wannsee in January 1945. After being found guilty by the People's Court, on 2 March, he was sentenced to death. In pursuance of Hitler's orders for the would-be assassins to 'hanged like cattle', Nebe was hanged in Berlin's Plötzensee Prison from a meat hook with a strand of piano wire.

Commander of Einsatzgruppe A, SS-Standartenführer Karl Jäger, who in 1942 had infamously declared the Baltic States 'Judenfrei' – free of Jews – then also sought medical assistance for depression.

SS supreme commander, Central Russia, SS-Obergruppenführer Erich von dem Bach-Zelewski, was another who developed psychological issues as the bloody massacre of hundreds of thousands of Jews continued in Belorussia. For three months in mid-1941, he supervised the extermination work of Einsatzgruppe B's *Aktion* programme, under SS-Gruppenführer Arthur Nebe, in Minsk and Riga. He also visited mass-murder sites at Bialystok, Grodno, Baranovichi, Mogilev and Pinsk.

Bach-Zelewski must have been one of the most cold-hearted and pitiless of Hitler's henchmen, but in February 1942, he suffered a nervous breakdown and was hospitalized: the genocide had resulted in hallucinations.

As the mental health of his death-squad troops escalated and increasing numbers were being returned to Berlin, Himmler grew concerned about his capabilities to bring the 'Final Solution' to its desired conclusion. By the end of 1942, locally recruited auxiliaries outnumbered German members of the Einsatzgruppen by ten to one. More efficient ways of exterminating the eastern European Jews had to be devised, especially in a way that would significantly reduce individual exposure to the actual job of killing.

Notwithstanding this problem, the confinement in and subsequent liquidation of Jewish ghettos peaked in 1942. In the summer of that year, the genocide entered a 'second wave' of calculated and systematic killings. While the programme facilitated the creaming off of able-bodied men to work in the labour camps, on average 90 per cent of ghetto inhabitants were slaughtered in mass shootings by the Einsatzgruppen. By mid-1943, the Jewish communities had been largely exterminated, and the Einsatzgruppen diverted their attention to the elimination of non-Jewish Soviet civilians – the despised Bolsheviks.

Hitler had also turned his focus to the west, where he knew that the mass-shooting methodology employed in Eastern Europe to address the Jewish 'problem' would attract undesirable levels of revulsion and condemnation from the West. Added to this, Hitler was cognizant of the low morale in his SS, and knew the Jewish pogrom in Western Europe would have to be far less hands-on.

On 20 January 1942, in a luxurious villa on Wannsee, near Berlin, Heydrich, Eichmann and other top SS and SD officers met to review the Einsatzgruppen reports on the status of the Final Solution in Eastern Europe. Of significance, however, was their intention to formulate a plan for the eradication of Jews in Western Europe. To achieve this, there was a consensus that they should be railed to extermination camps in the east. These 'death factories' would be equipped to gas large numbers of Jews – place names that would forever be memorialized in the dark annals of mankind: Auschwitz, Majdanek, Bełżec, Sobibór, Treblinka, Chełmno, Stutthof.

Operation Reinhard, named in honour of the assassinated Heydrich, was conceived.

The camps were erected under the auspices of the Reichskommissariat Ostland, the General Government of Ostland, comprising the German-occupied territories of the Baltic States, northeast Poland, and western Belorussia. Governor-General Hans Frank's loathing of the Jewish race knew no bounds. The former personal lawyer to Hitler, who would become a leading player in the Holocaust, vented his hatred in a public address: 'These hooked-nosed predators, these messengers of destruction, these pitiful pipsqueaks and buffoons of darkness, these accursed scum! Germans don't like Jews; Jews don't like Germans. So the Jew must disappear!'

However, the strength and spread of Hitler's military prowess had reached its zenith, and appeared to be losing momentum. Two simultaneous defining events

Himmler (centre) on a visit to the Mauthausen-Gusen concentration camp complex near Linz, Upper Austria. (Photo Bundesarchiv)

literally denied Hitler the means to fuel his dream of an Aryan world free of Jews and Bolsheviks: failure to seize the vast oilfields in Eastern Europe, and those in North Africa and the Middle East.

In August 1942, Lieutenant-General Bernard Montgomery assumed command of the Eighth Army in the Western Desert of North Africa. From 23 October to 11 November, the Allies pushed ailing Generalfeldmarschall Erwin Rommel's combined Afrika Korps and Italian forces 700 miles west toward Tunisia, thereby securing the strategic oilfields to the east. Himmler's plan to deploy Einsatzkommando Ägypten (Egypt) was shelved. The unit, under SS-Obersturmbannführer Walther Rauff, was to have been a mobile death squad to eliminate Jews in Palestine.

On 22 November, Generalfeldmarschall Friedrich Paulus, commander of the German Sixth Army, informed Berlin that his forces had been enveloped by the Red Army (Operation Uranus) just to the west of the beleaguered Stalingrad. Paulus needed a minimum of 750 tons of provisions a day to keep his twenty entrapped German and two Rumanian divisions from starving in the freezing blizzards of the southern-steppe winter. In the comfort of his heated headquarters, Hitler forbade any talk of Paulus breaking out to the southwest to link up with the Fourth Panzer Army deployed to go to Paulus's aid: 'Surrender is forbidden. Sixth Army will hold their positions to the last man and the last round and by their heroic endurance will make an

---

The Chief of the Security Police and the SD Berlin
February 25, 1942

Einsatzgruppe A
Location: Krasnogvardeisk
In the course of a routine Security Police screening of an additional part of the civilian population around Leningrad, 140 more people had to be shot. The reasons for this were as follows:

  a) Active participation in the Communist Party before the arrival of the German troops;
  b) Seditious and provocative activity since the arrival of the German Army;
  c) Partisan activity;
  d) Espionage;
  e) Belonging to the Jewish race.

Einsatzgruppe C
Location: Kiev
During the period January 14 to February 12, 1942, 861 people were shot by order of the Summary Court by Sonderkommando 4b. Of this number, 649 were political officials, 52 saboteurs and partisans, and 139 Jews.

The number of Summary Court shootings carried out by Einsatzkommando 5 during the period January 12 to January 24, 1942 totalled 104 political officials, 75 saboteurs and looters, and about 8,000 Jews. In the past weeks, Einsatzkommando 6 shot 173 political officials, 56 saboteurs and looters, and 149 Jews.

During the period January 10 to February 6, 1942, in Dniepropetrovsk, 17 habitual criminals, 103 Communist officials, 16 partisans, and about 350 Jews were shot by order of the Summary Court.

In addition, 400 inmates of the Igrin mental hospital and 320 inmates of the Vasilkova mental hospital were disposed of.

---

unforgettable contribution toward the establishment of a defensive front and the salvation of the Western world.'

As it transpired, the German armour's attempt – Operation Winter Storm – to relieve Paulus failed, leaving 300,000 men to fate. Between 31 January and 2 February 1943, Paulus sustained 147,000 killed and wounded and 91,000 taken prisoner, including twenty-four generals. Of this number, a mere 5,000 survived the Soviet labour camps to return to Germany after the war. Hitler declared four days of national mourning, but he would have been more likely to rue the failure to eradicate the loathsome Bolsheviks, thereby denying him access to the oil-rich Caucasus.

Shortly before his assassination in May 1942, Heydrich placed SS-Standartenführer Paul Blobel, commander of Einsatzkommando 4a, of Einsatzgruppe C, in charge of Sonderaktion, or Special Action 1005. Also – more accurately – known as *enterdungaktion*, or exhumation action, Blobel commenced his task in May, starting with the eradication of evidence of Operation Reinhard, the revenge massacre of thousands for the assassination of Heydrich. Sonderkommando 1005, raised solely for the cover up, included shackled prisoner work groups called *leichenkommandos* (corpse units) who were tasked with exhuming bodies and burning them. At the Chełmno extermination camp, near the Polish villages of Chełmno and Nerem, Blobel experimented with incendiary bombs to destroy exhumed bodies, but the results were unsatisfactory and set fire to adjoining forests. He then resorted to massive pyres, in which alternate layers of corpses and firewood were stacked on iron grids and set alight. Remaining bones were ground up, and the ashes buried. Once done, the prisoners employed to perform the gruesome dirty work were executed. A year later, the *Aktion* moved into the German-occupied territories in Eastern Europe to remove evidence of the Final Solution genocide.

In April 1943, the remains of 4,500 bodies were discovered by the Germans in Katyn Forest, the first of a total of 25,000 Polish army officer POWs and professionals murdered by the NKVD under orders from Stalin and the politburo. Other such sites included Kharkov, Miednoje, Kozielsk, Starobielsk and Ostaszków.

For Hitler, this proved to be a useful propaganda coup to drive a wedge between the Soviet Union and her western Allies, but the overt apportioning of blame between Hitler and Stalin rang warning bells in the Führer's toxic brain. This galvanized the dictator to place the mechanism to remove all traces of his genocide directly under Nazi leadership. The exercise proved to be extremely time-consuming, a reflection of the magnitude of the genocide. As a consequence, not all massacre sites could be sanitized, especially as the Red Army was pushing the Germans back to Germany.

Memorial to Polish POWs and intellectuals murdered on the orders of Joseph Stalin, Cannock Chase, England. The Nazis used the massacres to foment Polish hatred against Soviet Jews.

In July 1943, Generalfeldmarschall Erich von Manstein acted on Hitler's orders to execute a strategic offensive against Kursk, codenamed Operation Citadel. The Germans pitted 781,000 troops and 3,000 tanks against Soviet Marshal Konstantin Rokossovsky's force of 1.9 million men and 5,100 tanks. But Hitler's war machine was no longer invincible. Having prevented the Germans from breaking their front, the Red Army launched Operation Kutuzova, a successful but costly counter-offensive to the north. To the south, the Red Army's Operation Polkovodets Rumyantsev initially met obstinate resistance from German armour, but it would be in the second half of August before the Kursk campaign could be claimed by the Kremlin as a fundamental strategic victory – the Nazis had at last been turned.

The landmark battle significantly heightened the urgency that Hitler felt to ensure that all traces of the eastern European massacres were obliterated. His thousand-year Reich was slipping away from him, and with it the complacency that, with time, no one would remember what the Einsatzgruppen had done in Eastern Europe.

The sanitizing exercise continued well into 1944, following the same methodology: bring in squads of Jewish prisoners and erect barbed-wire encampments in which they slept at night during the exhumation stage, burn the bodies, bury the ashes, shoot the prisoners, move on. It was not uncommon for fresh executions to take place at the same time, the bodies burned with those that had been exhumed. The stench of burning corpses that had been in the ground for two to three years permeated the forests and the noses and lungs of all those in the vicinity.

In Kaunas, the second largest city in Lithuania, Sonderaktion 1005 concentrated their efforts on the Ninth Fort, the site where 80,000 Jews had been murdered and buried by the Einsatzkommandos. The fort was a pre-First World War addition to eight forts and nine gun emplacements constructed in the late nineteenth century under the orders of Tsar Nicholas II to defend Russia's western border. In 1924, Ninth Fort was converted into the Kaunas City Prison. When Lithuania fell to the Germans, Ninth Fort became a collection staging point for Jews facing execution, earning it the sobering title of 'Death Fort'. Arriving on 23 October 1943, the 1005 task force used Lithuanian partisan prisoners to exhume and burn the corpses. Thousands of women and babies were disinterred, the latter referred to as 'dolls' by the Germans. Facial recognition had become impossible.

The kommandos were meticulous in the execution of their task, with each assigned a specific role: the *brandmeister* had to feed the fire, while the *zähler* counted and recorded the corpses carefully stacked on the pyre. On occasion, phosphorus was added to the fires for greater heat.

With the collapse of the German Eastern Front, the SS and SD visited a frenzied orgy of fire and death on the civilians as they retreated – scorched earth would be the valedictory gift of the defeated conqueror.

In the spring of 1944, SS divisions on the crumbling Eastern Front were redeployed to the west. In Belgium, France and Italy, the death squads brought their genocidal 'skills' with them. In a June 1944 Einsatzgruppen 92 report, the massacres by elements of the 2nd SS 'Das Reich' Division of civilians in the French villages of Tulle and Oradour-sur-Glane are recorded. The division had participated in the genocide activities of Einsatzgruppe B in the rural areas of Belorussia.

Commanded by SS-Gruppenführer Heinz Lammerding, the division reassembled in the south of France near Toulouse, from where they were deployed to a 50-mile region from Tulle northwest to Limoges to eradicate French resistance fighters, the Maquis Francs-Tireurs et Partisans (FTP) of Corrèze.

Early on 7 June, several hundred *maquisards* attacked the 600-strong Wehrmacht garrison, and by late morning they had secured the train station and several key buildings used by the Germans. The following afternoon, in confusing circumstances that remain unclear, German troops who were trying to leave were killed at close range by rifle fire and hand grenades, resulting in horrifically mutilated bodies. Most of the more than fifty prisoners were also executed and the town reoccupied by the Maquis.

That night, the 'Das Reich' armour arrived and restored German control of the town. On the morning of 9 June, SS-Sturmbannführer Aurel Kowatsch ordered the rounding up of all men between the ages of 16 and 60 to facilitate the selection of those believed to have 'committed the crime against our comrades in the Tulle garrison'. Spokesman for the SD kommandos, Walter Schmald, selected 120 men based entirely on their appearance, contending that the unshaven and dishevelled were responsible. At around 3.30 p.m., declaring that they had perfected hanging in Kiev and Kharkov in the Ukraine, they commenced the systematic hanging of the victims. Executing ten at a time, the nooses suspended from lampposts, trees and balconies, were placed on the prisoners and the ladders kicked out from beneath them. The executions were sped up by SS troops hanging from the victims' legs or by shooting them. Ninety-nine perished, while most of those who had been rounded up were deported to the Compiègne internment camp in northern France, or to Dachau concentration camp, where few survived.

Oradour-sur-Glane. The ruins of the village remain untouched since its destruction and the massacre of its citizens by the SS on 10 June 1944. (Photo John Pollard)

On 10 June, as the Allies struggled to gain a bloody beachhead on the Normandy coast, SS – Sturmbannführer Adolf Diekmann, commanding the 3rd Company, 1st Battalion, 4th SS-Panzergrenadier Regiment, surrounded Oradour-sur-Glane around noon. After herding the residents into the marketplace and sorting them in groups of gender and age, 197 men were taken away and locked inside barns on the outskirts of the village. The barns were then set ablaze, and anyone who managed to escape the inferno was immediately shot. At the same time, 240 women and 205 children were locked inside the village church and hand grenades lobbed through the windows.

Only seven of the 642 victims were Jewish. Only six men and one women survived. At 8 p.m., after thoroughly looting the village, the Germans razed Oradour-sur-Glane to the ground before leaving. Diekmann would never answer to the crime as he was killed in action three weeks later.

Three years after the 9–13 December 1941 massacre at Simferopol in the Crimea, in which SS-Gruppenführer Dr Otto Ohlendorf's Einsatzgruppe D murdered over 10,000 civilians, predominantly Jewish, on 13 March 1944 a further *aktion* was carried out by the retreating Germans to erase the evidence.

Allied aerial bombardment and the advancing Red Army from the east eventually crushed the Third Reich by the end of April 1945. On 2 April 1945, only weeks before taking his own life in his underground bunker, Adolf Hitler remained defiant and boastfully philosophical: 'In a world where the moral order is increasingly contaminated by the Jewish poison, a people immunized against it will someday recover its superiority. From this point of view, eternal gratitude will be due to National Socialism because I have exterminated the Jews in Germany and in Central Europe.' ('Einsatzgruppen, The Death Brigades', PBS America)

Babi Yar ravine. (Photo Mark Voorendt)

5. THIS WORLD'S BIGGEST MURDER CASE

'The naked people stepped down the stairs carved in the pit's wall, and walked over the heads of those who lay there to the spot where the SS man told them. Then they lowered themselves atop of the dead or those who were still alive. A volley of shots was heard. I looked into the pit and saw the stirring bodies and the bodies down below which didn't stir. Blood was running from the back of their necks.'

From the testimony before the International Military Tribunal in Nuremberg of Herman Friedrich Graebe, director of the Ukraine branch of the Jung company, about what he had witnessed in Dubno, Volhynia, on 5 October 1942

Officially convening the public war crimes trial at Nuremberg on 20 November 1945, British President of the International Tribunal, Lord Justice Geoffrey Lawrence, said, 'The trial which is now to begin ... is of supreme importance to millions of people all over the globe.'

Sitting between 1945 and 1949, the tribunal initially heard the most famous cases – the major war criminals – from 21 November 1945 to 1 October 1946.

By the cessation of hostilities in Europe in 1945, the Allies had already become aware of heinous atrocities that had taken place in Eastern Europe – the Holocaust. The imperative then for the Allies was to expeditiously bring those responsible, as well as those who had waged war, to account.

The city of Nuremberg was chosen for the trials as it had been the venue of the infamous Nazi mass rallies. By establishing the tribunal there, it would emphasise the final demise of German National Socialism. Furthermore, the spacious Palace of Justice had largely escaped Allied bombing and also housed a large prison within the complex.

The first trials at Nuremberg were for twenty-four senior Nazis, charged with some or all of:

1) Participation in a common plan or conspiracy for the accomplishment of crime against peace.
2) Planning, initiating and waging wars of aggression and other crime against peace.
3) War Crimes
4) Crimes against humanity.

Hermann Göring, Karl Dönitz and Rudolf Hess at the Nuremberg war crimes trials. (Photo US Army Signals Corps)

Following the trials of the Nazi hierarchy, including Martin Bormann, Karl Dönitz, Hermann Göring, Rudolph Hess, Alfred Jodl, Wilhelm Keitel, Albert Speer and Joachim von Ribbentrop, the United States conducted a series of twelve US military tribunals for war crimes. Generally referred to as the 'subsequent Nuremberg trials', the US trials took place in the same rooms at the Palace of Justice in Nuremberg.

Twenty-four former officers of the SS Einsatzgruppen mobile death squads were convicted in Case No. 9 – the 'Einsatzgruppen Trial' – which was held before the International Military Tribunal from 27 September 1947 to 9 April 1948. In its judgement in this case, the tribunal stated: 'In this case the defendants are not simply accused of planning or directing wholesale killings through channels. They are not charged with sitting in an office hundreds and thousands of miles away from the slaughter. It is asserted with particularity that these men were in the field actively superintending, controlling, directing, and taking an active part in the bloody harvest.'

All were found guilty. Fourteen were sentenced to death, twelve had their sentences commuted, one committed suicide during the trial, and the remainder were sentenced to various terms of imprisonment:

- Otto Ohlendorf: SS-Gruppenführer, member of the SD, commanding officer of Einsatzgruppe D. Sentenced to death and hanged at Landsberg Prison in Bavaria on 8 June 1951.
- Heinz Jost: SS-Brigadeführer, member of the SD, commanding officer of Einsatzgruppe A. Sentenced to life imprisonment, subsequently commuted to ten years. Released from Landsberg prison in 1951. He then worked in Düsseldorf as a real estate agent. Died at Bensheim in 1964.
- Erich Naumann: SS-Brigadeführer, member of the SD, commanding officer of Einsatzgruppe B. Sentenced to death and hanged on 8 June 1951.
- Dr Otto Rasch: SS-Brigadeführer, member of the SD and the Gestapo, commanding officer of Einsatzgruppe C. Trial discontinued on 5 February 1948 because he suffered from Parkinson's disease and related dementia. Died on 1 November that year in Wehrstedt, Lower Saxony.
- Erwin Schulz: SS-Brigadeführer, member of the Gestapo, commanding officer of Einsatzkommando 5 of Einsatzgruppe C. Sentenced to twenty years' imprisonment, subsequently commuted to fifteen years. Released from Landsberg prison in 1954. Died in 1981.
- Walter Blume: SS-Standartenführer, member of the SD and the Gestapo, commanding officer of Sonderkommando 7a of Einsatzgruppe B. Sentenced to death, subsequently commuted to twenty-five years. Released in 1955 and died in 1974. In 1997, a horde of top-quality watches, rings, gold bars and gold teeth worth approximately $4 million, together with identity documents and Gestapo promotions belonging to Walter Blume were discovered in Brazil in the possession of a family member, pawnbroker Albert Blume.
- Dr Franz Six: SS-Brigadeführer, member of the SD, commanding officer of Vorkommando Moscow of Einsatzgruppe B. Sentenced to twenty years' imprisonment, subsequently commuted to ten years. Released in 1952 when he found work as an advertising executive for Porsche. Died in 1975 in Bolzano, Italy.
- Paul Blobel: SS-Standartenführer, member of the SD, commanding officer of Sonderkommando 4a of Einsatzgruppe C. Sentenced to death and hanged on 8 June 1951.
- Lothar Fendler: SS-Sturmbannführer, member of the SD, deputy chief of Sonderkommando 4b of Einsatzgruppe C. Sentenced to ten years' imprisonment,

subsequently commuted to eight years. Released from Landsberg Prison in 1951. Date of death unknown.

- Eugen Steimle: SS-Standartenführer, member of the SD, commanding officer of Sonderkommando 7a of Einsatzgruppe B and Sonderkommando 4a of Einsatzgruppe C. Sentenced to death, subsequently commuted to twenty years. Released from Landsberg Prison in 1954, he then went on to teach German and history in Wilhelmsdorf, Baden-Württemberg. Retired in 1975 and died in 1987.
- Ernst Biberstein: SS-Obersturmbannführer, member of the SD, commanding officer of Einsatzkommando 6 of Einsatzgruppe C. Sentenced to death, subsequently commuted to life imprisonment. Released in 1958 and temporarily returned to being a Protestant pastor. Died in 1986 in Neumünster.
- Willy Seibert: SS-Standartenführer, member of the SD, deputy chief of Einsatzgruppe D. Sentenced to death, subsequently commuted to fifteen years. Died in 1976.
- Gustav Nosske: SS-Obersturmbannführer, member of the Gestapo, commanding officer of Einsatzkommando 12 of Einsatzgruppe D. Sentenced to life imprisonment, subsequently commuted to ten years. Died in 1990.
- Adolf Ott : SS-Obersturmbannführer, member of the SD, commanding officer of Sonderkommando 7b of Einsatzgruppe B. Sentenced to death, subsequently commuted to life imprisonment. Released in 1958.
- Waldemar Klingelhöfer: SS-Sturmbannführer, member of the SD, officer of Sonderkommando 7b of Einsatzgruppe B. Sentenced to death, subsequently commuted to life imprisonment. Released in 1956 from Landsberg prison. In 1960, he was living in Villingen where he worked as an office clerk. Died around 1980.
- Dr Eduard Strauch: SS-Obersturmbannführer, member of the SD, commanding officer of Einsatzkommando 2 of Einsatzgruppe A. Sentenced to death. Handed over to authorities in Belgium to stand trial, where he was again sentenced to death, but the sentence was never carried out. Died in Belgian custody in 1955 in a hospital in Uccle.
- Mattias Graf: SS-Untersturmführer, member of the SD, officer in Einsatzkommando 6 of Einsatzgruppe D. Sentence served.
- Dr Werner Braune: SS-Obersturmbannführer, member of the SD and the Gestapo, commanding officer of Sonderkommando 11b of Einsatzgruppe D. Sentenced to death and hanged on 8 June 1951.
- Walter Hänsch: SS-Obersturmbannführer, member of the SD, commanding officer of Sonderkommando 4b of Einsatzgruppe C. Sentenced to death, subsequently commuted to fifteen years.

- Martin Sandberger: SS-Standartenführer, member of the SD, commanding officer of Sonderkommando 1a of Einsatzgruppe A. Sentenced to death, subsequently commuted to life imprisonment. Released from Landsberg prison in 1958. Died in 2010, aged 98.
- Waldemar von Radetzsky: SS-Sturmbannführer, member of the SD, Deputy chief of Sonderkommando 4a of Einsatzgruppe C. Sentenced to twenty years' imprisonment and released.
- Felix Rühl: SS-Hauptsturmführer, member of the Gestapo, officer of Sonderkommando 10b of Einsatzgruppe D. Sentenced to ten years' imprisonment and released.
- Heinz Schübert: SS-Obersturmführer, member of the SD, officer in Einsatzgruppe D. Sentenced to death, subsequently commuted to ten years. Released in 1952.
- Emil Hausmann: SS-Sturmbannführer, member of the SD, officer of Einsatzkommando 12 of Einsatzgruppe D. On 31 July 1947, he committed suicide in his holding cell at Nuremberg, the only defendant at the Einsatzgruppen trial to escape justice.

Otto Ohlendorf, his duty to his Führer loyally fulfilled, gave his own account of his reactions to the gruesome tasks that he had undertaken. He stated how he had received his initial orders, along with the other Einsatzgruppen commanders, from two SS colonels only three days before he deployed to the front:

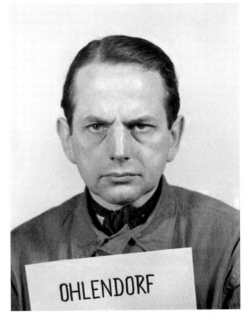

The immediate feeling with me and with the other men was one of general protest. Colonel Streckenbach told us that even he himself had protested most strenuously against a similar order during the Polish campaign, but that Himmler had rebuked him just as severely by stating that this was a Fuhrer-order which must be carried out.

Otto Ohlendorf, commander Einsatzgruppe D, on trial at Nuremberg, charged with being responsible for the massacre of 90,000 men, women and children, predominantly Jewish.

I did not consider the order justified because quite independently from the necessity of taking such measures, they would have moral consequences which would result in a deterioration of the mind.

But I had as little possibility as any of the others to prevent this order. There was only one thing, a senseless martyrdom through suicide, senseless because this would not have changed anything in the execution of this order. For it was not an order of the SS, it was an order of the Supreme Commander-in-Chief and the Head of State. It was not only carried out by Himmler and Heydrich. The Army had to carry it out too, the High Command of the Army as well as the commanders in the East and South-East who were the Supreme Commanders of the Action Groups [Einsatzgruppen].

History of the Second World War, Vol. 3, No. 9

GUNS GUARD JAIL AS SEVEN NAZIS ARE EXECUTED

The last seven major Nazi war criminals, sentenced to death three years ago, were hanged in Landsberg prison early today. Three times earlier the executions had been postponed – twice after the graves had been dug. U.S. troops with machine guns and fixed bayonets were on duty outside the jail, but there were no demonstrations. Up to the last the Landsberg seven, sentenced for the mass murder or torture of 280,000 hoped for reprieve or stay of execution.

The men were:

Otto Ohlendorf, whose extermination squads killed about 90,000 people.

Oswald Pohl, blamed for destroying the Warsaw ghetto and exterminating or deporting 66,000 Jews.

Paul Blobel, who ordered the killing of 60,000 Jews.

Werner Braune and Erich Naumann, each blamed for massacring thousands of Jews and gipsies.

Hans Schmidt, who supervised Buchenwald concentration camp executions; and

George Schallermair, who killed large numbers of prisoners at another concentration camp.

Yorkshire Evening Post, Thursday, 7 June 1951

SS-Obergruppenführer Erich von dem Bach-Zelewski, who had overseen the extermination of Jews in Riga and Minsk by Einsatzgruppe B, commanded by Arthur Nebe, gave evidence for the prosecution and was never put on trial for war crimes. He was briefly imprisoned until 1949, but two years later he was sentenced to ten years imprisonment for murdering political opponents in the 1930s.

However, he only went to prison in 1958 after being convicted and sentenced to four and a half years for the murder of fellow SS officer SS–Obersturmführer Anton von Hohberg und Buchwald in July 1934.

Bach-Zelewski gave evidence for the defence at the trial of Adolf Eichmann in Israel in May 1961, the same year in which he was sentenced to an additional ten years in prison for the murder of six German communists in the early 1930s. He never faced extradition to either Poland or the Soviet Union, and died in a Munich prison on 8 March 1972.

In 1943, in the immediate wake of the departure of the German invaders, the Soviet judicial system asserted itself in liberated areas to bring war criminals to trial. The first of many such courts was held in Kharkov in the Ukraine where, in a ravine outside the town of Drobytsky Yar, 15,000 predominantly Jews had been murdered in December 1941.

In 1946, a Soviet war crimes trial at Kiev in the Ukraine sat to hear evidence relating to the largest mass killing perpetrated by the Germans during their occupation of the city. In just two days, 29–30 September 1941, almost 34,000 Jewish residents of Kiev were slaughtered. SS-Obergruppenführer Friedrich Jeckeln, commander of Einsatzgruppe C, SS-Brigadeführer und Generalmajor der Polizei Dr Otto Rasch, Einsatzkommando SS-Standartenführer Paul Blobel, along with elements of the SD and SS and local police were responsible.

Dina Pronicheva, a survivor of the Babi Yar massacre in a ravine near the city, gave her evidence:

> They didn't undress us because it was already dark. They took us to the edge of the ravine [*yar*]. We could hardly stand. They started to shoot. I closed my eyes and clenched my fists. I tensed my muscles and let myself fall in the pit. After what seemed like forever, I landed on some bodies. Some were only wounded.
>
> Later the shooting stopped, and I heard the Germans climb down into the ravine to shoot the ones who were suffocating. They had flashlights to see who was still alive. I kept lying there. I stayed as still as I could, so they wouldn't spot me. I thought my end had come. I waited in silence.

They began covering the bodies with soil. I was covered in soil and felt I was suffocating. I was afraid to move. I only had a few gulps of air to go before suffocating. I'd preferred being shot to dying of suffocation.

I started to move. I didn't realize it was so dark. I freed my left hand. I got my breath back and washed away the soil. After taking a few breaths, using what strength remained, I got out from under the earth. It was night time, but it was dangerous to move because the Germans were lighting the pit from above. They were still shooting the wounded and could've hit me. So I had to be very careful.

I managed to creep to the walls of the ravine, and with a superhuman effort, I hoisted myself out.

> From Russian archival film of the trial,
> *Einsatzgruppen: The Death Brigades*, PBS America

Friedrich Jeckeln, commander of one of the largest collections of Einsatzgruppen and personally responsible for ordering and organizing the deaths of over 100,000 Jews, Slavs, gypsies and other racial 'misfits', was taken prisoner by Soviet troops near Halbe on 28 April 1945. Along with other German personnel who served in the Riga military district, he was tried before a Soviet military tribunal in Riga, Latvia, from 26 January 1946 to 3 February 1946. During the trial, he was composed, answering questions from investigators with measured restraint. Finally, he accepted full responsibility for his personal activities as well as those of the SS and SD in Ostland: 'I have to take full responsibility for what happened in the borders of Ostland, within SS, SD and the Gestapo. Thereby increases much my fault. My fate is in the hands of the High Court, and so I ask only to pay attention to mitigating circumstances. I will accept a sentence in full repentance and I will consider as worthy punishment.'

Jeckeln and the other defendants were found guilty, sentenced to death and hanged in Uzvaras Laukums (Victory Square) in Riga, Latvia, on 3 February 1946, in front of some 4,000 onlookers.

Evidence presented at Nuremberg by Paul Blobel regarding the burning of bodies and obliterating the traces of bodies of Jews killed by the Einsatzgruppen, is contained in Affidavit NO-3947, Nuremberg, 18 June 1947:

I, Paul Blobel, swear, declare and state in evidence:

1. I was born in Potsdam on August 13, 1894. From June 1941 to January 1942, I was the Commander of Sonderkommando 4 A [Einsatzgruppe C].

2. After I had been released from this command, I was to report in Berlin to SS Obergruppenführer Heydrich and Gruppenführer [Heinrich] Mueller, and

Paul Blobel, commander
Einsatzgruppe C, charged at
Nuremberg with the murder of
almost 34,000 Jews in Kiev.

in June 1942 I was entrusted by Gruppenführer Mueller with the task of obliterating the traces of executions carried out by the Einsatzgruppen in the East.

My orders were that I should report in person to the commanders of the Security Police and SD, pass on Mueller's orders verbally, and supervise their implementation. This order was top secret, and Gruppenführer Mueller had given orders that owing to the need for strictest secrecy there was to be no correspondence in connection with this task.

In September 1942 I reported to Dr. Thomas in Kiev and passed the order on to him. The order could not be carried out immediately, partly because Dr. Thomas was disinclined to carry it out, and also because the materials required for the burning of the bodies were not available. In May and June 1943, I made additional trips to Kiev in this matter and then, after conversations with Dr. Thomas and with SS and Police Leader Hennecke, the order was carried out.

3. During my visit in August I myself observed the burning of bodies in a mass grave near Kiev. This grave was about 55 m. long, 3 m. wide and 2½ m. deep. After the top had been removed the bodies were covered with inflammable

material and ignited. It took about two days until the grave burned down to the bottom. I myself observed that the fire had glowed down to the bottom. After that the grave was filled in and the traces were now practically obliterated.

4. Owing to the moving up of the front-line it was not possible to destroy the mass graves further south and east which had resulted from executions by the Einsatzgruppen. I travelled to Berlin in this connection to report, and was then sent to Estonia by Gruppenführer Mueller. I passed on the same orders to Oberführer Achammer-Pierader in Riga, and also to Obergruppenführer Jeckeln. I returned to Berlin in order to obtain fuel. The burning of the bodies began only in May or June 1944. I remember that incinerations took place in the area of Riga and Reval. I was present at such incinerations near Reval, but the graves were smaller here and contained only about 20 to 30 bodies. The graves in the area of Reval were about 20 or 30 km east of the city in a marshy district and I think that 4 or 5 such graves were opened and the bodies burned.

5. According to my orders I should have extended my duties over the entire area occupied by the Einsatzgruppen, but owing to the retreat from Russia I could not carry out my orders completely.

    I have made this disposition of my own free will, without any kind of promise of reward, and I was not subjected to any form of compulsion or threat.
    Signed Paul Blobel

SS-Obersturmbannführer Otto Adolf Eichmann, grand architect of Jewish affairs, ghettos and deportation to extermination camps – a mass extension of the initial rounding up and murder conducted by the Einsatzgruppen – avoided capture and escaped to South America. In May 1960, Mossad (Israeli Intelligence and Special Operations) agents abducted Eichmann in Buenos Aires, from where he was flown to Israel where he stood trial for war crimes. In December 1961, he was found guilty and sentenced to death by hanging. Eichmann was hanged in Ramleh Prison, near Tel Aviv, just after midnight on 1 June 1962, his body immediately cremated, and the ashes thrown into the Mediterranean outside Israeli territorial waters.

Throughout, Eichmann remained defiant and showed no contrition:

How much time fate allows me to live, I do not know. I do know that someone must inform this generation and the next about the happenings of my era. I am writing this story at a time when I am in full possession of my physical and mental freedom, influenced or pressed by no one. May future historians be objective enough not to stray from the path of the true facts recorded here.

During the first Nurnberg trial, my most trusted subordinate testified against me. So did others. Perhaps these people referred to me in order to whitewash themselves. But when such a thing goes on for years and everyone joins in, thus fixing the blame for past deeds, a legend is created in which exaggeration plays a large part.

In actual fact, I was merely a little cog in the machinery that carried out the directives and orders of the German Reich. I am neither a murderer nor a mass-murderer. I am a man of average good qualities, and many faults. I was not the 'czar of the Jews' as a Paris newspaper once called me, nor was I responsible for all the good and evil deeds done against them. Where I was implicated in the physical annihilation of the Jews, I admit my participation freely and without pressure. After all, I was the one who transported the Jews to the camps. If I had not transported them, they would never have been delivered to the butcher.

Yet what is there to 'admit?' I carried out my orders. It would be as pointless to blame me for the whole Final Solution of the Jewish Problem as to blame the minister who was in charge of the railroads over which the Jewish transports travelled.

But with us an order was an order. If I had sabotaged the order of the one-time Fuhrer of the German Reich, Adolf Hitler, I would have been not only a scoundrel but a despicable dog, like those who broke their military oath to join the ranks of the anti-Hitler criminals in the conspiracy of July 20, 1944.

At the Nurnberg trials, the world was given a new interpretation of justice. Not one Russian, no Israeli, no Englishman or North American was punished in even a single instance because he carried out commands given to him while he was in an official position or under military oath. Why should the gallows or the penitentiary be reserved for Germans only?

After assuming a false identity as Sergeant, Heinrich Hitzinger in the German army, on 21 May 1945 Heinrich Himmler was identified and arrested at a checkpoint near the town of Bremerforde. Two days later, at the British 31st Civilian Interrogation Camp near Lüneburg, while under medical examination, he bit into a cyanide pill. Fifteen minutes later he was dead, cheating justice.

Father of the Einsatzgruppen death squads, SS-Reichsführer Heinrich Luitpold Himmler, four years earlier – to the day – formalized his intention to raise units for deployment in newly occupied German territories in Eastern Europe to perform 'special tasks I shall give them'.

INDEX

Acknowledgements & Sources

My sincere thanks to friend and fellow military historian Dr Yagil Henkin, Professor IDF Command and General Staff College, Glilot, Israel, and for my introduction to Yad Vashem, memorial site home of the Holocaust History Museum in Jerusalem. The Jewish Virtual Library website was an invaluable source of original information on the Einsatzgruppen death squads' activities. The following sources proved invaluable: Central Intelligence Agency Office, *Study of Intelligence and Counterintelligence Activities on the Eastern Front and in Adjacent Areas During WWII.* (Released 1999); Central Intelligence Agency Office of Training, *Studies in Intelligence*, Vol. 4 No. 1, Winter 1960. (Released 2005) Peter Longerich, *Heinrich Himmler.* (Oxford University Press, New York, 2012); US Department of War, Strategic Services Unit, *The Career of Heinrich Himmler.* (Released by Central Intelligence Agency 2001).